Praise for *It Pays to Be Paranoid*

"Christopher Eiben has done the world of commerce an enormous service. He provides vivid examples of what can go wrong in the real world and solid advice on how to stay on the straight-and-narrow. If that weren't enough, *It Pays to Be Paranoid* is a wonderfully engaging read."

—Joseph T. Wells, CFE, CPA, founder and chairman,
Association of Certified Fraud Examiners

"Getting it right demands knowing what can go wrong. Christopher Eiben's *It Pays to Be Paranoid* provides the wisdom and guidance to avoid the risks of today's litigious society. For your own safety, sleep with it tucked beneath your pillow."

—Albert J. Weatherhead III, founder, Weatherhead School of Management,
Case Western Reserve University

"Stay out of court! Managers could avoid many a costly legal mess by watching their step beforehand. Christopher Eiben's clear case histories, based on hard-won experience, raise the right sorts of questions—and they're a lot less painful than paying lawyers after the fact."

—Walter K. Olson, author of *The Litigation Explosion*

"I wish I'd had the benefit of *It Pays to Be Paranoid* earlier in my business career. It could have saved me some heartache. Christopher Eiben has hit the right balance between being cautious and thorough on the one hand without being cynical or hard-hearted on the other."

—John D. Beckett, chairman, The Beckett Companies,
and author of *Loving Monday*

"*It Pays to Be Paranoid* is a scary but valuable read, emphasizing the critical importance of due-diligence when evaluating business opportunities and background investigations when evaluating people. Read this well-crafted book!"

—Robert L. Pool, past chairman, National Association for the Self Employed

"Christopher Eiben provides valuable lessons learned from his many years as a legal investigator, an indispensable guide for anyone owning a business, opening a business, or even thinking of opening a business."

—Rory McMahon, certified legal investigator, author of
The Practical Handbook for Private Investigators

"This book provides clear-sighted and cautionary lessons that illustrate the value of positive paranoia. Read it and learn how to avoid mistakes that can devastate a business."

—Loyal Wilson, managing director, Primus Venture Partners Inc.

"If forewarned is forearmed, readers of this book will be better prepared to meet the day-to-day hazards involved in pursuing the entrepreneurial ideal."

—Steve Millard, executive director, Council of Smaller Enterprises

It Pays to Be Paranoid

Securing Business Success by Preparing for the Worst

□ □ □

CHRISTOPHER EIBEN

Christopher Eiben hoc fecit MMV

AGATE

CHICAGO

Printed in Canada.

Library of Congress Cataloging-in-Publication Data

Eiben, Christopher J.
    It pays to be paranoid : securing business success by preparing for the worst / by Christopher Eiben.
       p.   cm.
    ISBN 1-932841-02-4 (pbk.)
    1. Risk management. 2. Risk assessment. 3. Fraud—Prevention. 4. Swindlers and swindling. I. Title.
    HD61.E38 2004
    658.4'7—dc22

                                   2004016232

10 9 8 7 6 5 4 3 2 1

Agate books are available in bulk at discount prices. For more information, go to agatepublishing.com.

Table of Contents

To Jaynie,
my beloved wife and talented editor.
This book is dedicated to you.

□ □ □

ACKNOWLEDGEMENTS

I would like to acknowledge my professional colleagues—members of the National Association of Legal Investigators and the Association of Certified Fraud Examiners—who generously helped and guided me on many cases over the years. Thanks also to Robert Healey, my friend and mentor, who strongly encouraged me to write this book.

CHAPTER 1

An Introduction to Positive Paranoia

"Learn from your mistakes" is an admonition for losers. Successful people learn from others' mistakes and thereby avoid their own.

As a professional investigator, I have seen countless businesspeople blunder into serious problems that consume their assets and upend their lives. Never once have I heard any of them say afterward, "I saw it coming." Instead, they almost always say in hindsight, "I *should* have seen it coming." Why do so many seemingly smart people make so many bad decisions that lead to catastrophic losses and lawsuits? Why are so many prone to the "big mistake"?

Americans are much admired for their optimism, their capacity to believe in themselves and in others. Boundless optimism has made our country the most entrepreneurial and innovative in the history of mankind. This optimism, however, can also be a deficiency, a kind of Achilles' heel that keeps otherwise sensible people from recognizing the potential for disaster. And the biggest disasters, as this book will demonstrate, are the two-legged variety. Misplaced trust in people causes more heartache and financial loss than all "acts of God" combined. People dutifully take shelter from an approaching electrical storm, but often fail to steer clear of the most obvious of scoundrels. Indeed, those who naively expect the best often find themselves saddled with the worst.

Like priests absolving sinners and psychiatrists treating the mentally disturbed, professional investigators like me look behind appearances and face the sad truth that many people are not nearly as moral, or as stable, or as upright as they appear to be. I am continually confronted with evidence that many people are not to be trusted and that our society, which equates money with success, breeds wrongdoing. The "winning is everything" values of today energize but also poison entrepreneurial activity, which then often metastasizes into villainy.

Over the years, I have seen hundreds of good people stumble into damaging relationships and bad business deals, oblivious to what they could have done to avoid them. Good intentions are not enough to stay trouble-free. Quite the contrary! Innocence often invites misfortune. Everyone—especially everyone in business—must be on guard and alert for trouble. Paranoia, after all, is perfectly sensible in a predatory world driven by the motivation to acquire as much money as quickly as possible. Unfortunately, acquiring money does not necessarily mean earning money. For the unscrupulous, hard work and frugality are not the preferred ways for getting ahead. There are quicker and more lucrative methods: extortion, embezzlement, financial fraud, theft, misappropriation of assets, contrived wrongful discharge and harassment claims, fraudulent workplace injuries, and many, many other imaginative strategies. With these ever-increasing perils, healthy skepticism has become a virtue in today's business world.

Misfortune, however, does not spring solely from the doings of the disreputable. Over the years, I have also seen countless cases where well-meaning people get dragged into costly disputes with other well-meaning people. Small mistakes and trivial gaffes often grow into outsized, life-altering controversies. Once entangled in an expensive and bewildering civil lawsuit, participants often feel the justice system conspires against them, which in fact it does. The wheels of justice, I believe, grind down everyone to varying degrees, with both the accused and the accuser getting damaged in every lawsuit, sometimes profoundly so. As an insider, I have witnessed many good people go through a hellish loss of innocence, experiencing emotional suffering almost as painful as losing a loved one. Self-incrimination compounds their distress during and after protracted legal battles. Traumatized courtroom survivors usually understand with perfect clarity that their ordeals could have been avoided or lessened simply by their being better prepared and more cautious beforehand.

How This Book Works

This book will tell some of these distressing stories and analyze the blunders involved. My aim is to teach readers the lessons these unfortunates had to learn the hard way. In addition to educating readers about specific business risks, I try to outline various prescriptive measures that (if followed) will help keep readers from making similar mistakes. Protection often means simply having the right policies and procedures in place before controversies arise. Written documentation and paper trails are often more valuable than insurance policies as protection from legal trouble.

Each chapter of this book begins with one or more case histories, followed by my critical analysis and some prescriptive guidelines. All of the cases I present here deal with authentic events and experiences, but names and other identifying information have been changed to protect identities and to keep me in compliance with state laws requiring licensed private investigators to maintain confidentiality. In addition, some of these cases are composites, combining different aspects of real-life events. I have tried to describe the true nitty-gritty of different kinds of business catastrophes and legal dramas, hoping the ugly details will help readers to be more mindful in their own lives. But no matter how vivid, these stories cannot truly convey how traumatizing and all-consuming real business and legal troubles can be. Lawsuits poison daily lives and cause debilitating worry. They often last for months and sometimes years as cases plod through arcane legal procedures and interminable legal maneuverings.

By writing this book, I hope to make readers more discerning about the underhanded ways some people use to take advantage of others. Problem-causing people will often appear to you as trustworthy partners, reliable employees, kind neighbors, and enthusiastic providers of goods and services. To avoid "the big mistake," you must become more cautious about where you place your trust. You must remain alert, protect your back, and keep your hand on your wallet. In short, you should pay attention to your paranoia!

Ironically, being wary and guarded increases significantly our chances for success and happiness. True success requires avoiding the bad and associating with the good. However, people often are not as they first appear and troublemakers generally are exposed only after they cause problems. The best way to disassociate from difficult people is to identify and steer clear of them in the first place.

But how do you recognize a saint from a sinner, particularly when hiring employees, evaluating investment deals, or considering business partnerships? How do you detect criminals, crackpots, slackers, thieves, and fraudsters *before* they cause you problems? The key is to investigate people thoroughly, always aware that initial impressions mean almost nothing in determining a person's worthiness. The only way to measure properly people's character, capacities, and tendencies is to look into their past.

While a background investigation is the best way to size up potential employees and partners, a due-diligence investigation is the best way to size up investment opportunities. Too often businesspeople enter into deals without asking enough questions beforehand, needlessly exposing themselves and their companies to significant financial risks. Business success requires good intelligence—having the right information to make reasoned business decisions. Without good intelligence, investments become crapshoots, with failure the likeliest outcome.

By following the principles and guidelines presented herein, readers should become more discerning in their dealings with others, thereby improving their odds for success. The goal, after all, is to associate with those who can literally and figuratively enrich our lives. Surrounding ourselves with good people increases our likelihood of happiness and peace of mind. But everyone—particularly businesspeople—will inevitably encounter troublemakers, despite their best efforts to be vigilant. Dealing effectively with these troublemakers requires decisiveness, forethought, and sound planning. In our increasingly litigious culture, fate favors the prepared more than ever.

CHAPTER 2

Due Diligence Before Starting, Buying, or Selling a Business

□ □ □ **CASE #1—VERNON YOST:**
"NO RISK, EASY MONEY"

There was never a nicer guy than Vernon Yost, a cheerful, almost childlike fellow who was always kind and helpful to those around him. A trusting soul, he reflexively thought well of everyone—which made him particularly vulnerable to the swindlers who took most of his life savings.

No one at the company where he worked had wanted to see Vernon take early retirement, but the financial incentives offered to vested employees were almost impossible to turn down. He received $45,000 in severance, continued health insurance coverage, and monthly retirement benefits calculated at 50 percent of his final pay scale. The retirement benefits, however, would not commence for three years, which was when he would turn sixty-two.

Handy at fixing things, Vernon had worked in his company's engineering department for more than thirty-three years. He liked to be useful and that was the problem. In the weeks after retiring, Vernon wandered aimlessly around his modest bungalow looking for something to do. When boredom began to dampen his natural enthusiasm and cheerfulness, he started scanning classified ads looking for a part-time job, knowing he'd drive himself and his wife crazy if he didn't get out of the house soon. Then one day he saw an advertisement that would transform his life.

> Position Available—Products Distributor
> Part-Time/Flexible Hours
> No Experience Required
> $1,500.00/week earning potential
> 1-800-XXX-Vend

Intrigued, Vernon called the number and reached a charming man who quickly put him at ease, though Vernon had some difficulty hearing him clearly over the many garbled telephone conversations going on in the background. This man, "Robby Jones," identified himself as the vice president of Vendor Opportunity Unlimited, a national company with a "cutting-edge" business plan that was "revolutionizing" the $40 billion per year vending industry. According to Robby, Vendor Opportunity Unlimited (Vend-Op for short) was looking for a "select few partners" to help grow its booming business. Vend-Op operated throughout the country through its hundreds of independent distributors, selling name-brand snacks from its patented vending machines. Most of its "distributors" managed anywhere from five to fifty vending machines located in high-traffic public places, such as bowling alleys and bus terminals, generating profits averaging $129 per week per machine. Robby knew of "scores" of distributors with just ten machines who made $150 per week per machine, hence the "$1,500 per week" earning potential identified in the advertisement.

Robby then explained to Vernon that Vend-Op was highly selective as to the "partners" it chose, and proceeded to ask Vernon about himself. Rather self-consciously, Vernon tried to put his best foot forward, outlining his work experience, various capabilities, and recent early retirement. After listening patiently, Robby observed that Vernon clearly had the mechanical aptitude necessary to maintain the machines, and his long employment with one company suggested his professional reliability. Nonetheless, Vernon would be required to complete an application and go through an approval process before he could become an authorized distributor. Impressed by Vernon's "business credentials," Robby promised to send him the application package by overnight delivery. He also promised to put in a good word on Vernon's behalf with the selection committee.

Robby went on to explain that all of the authorized distributors purchased their vending machines from Vend-Op, entitling them to "all the tax advantages of ownership." In turn, Vend-Op would provide "high-traffic" locations for the machines, comprehensive training, bulk discounts on name-brand snacks, money-back guarantees, and lifetime warranties. Vernon asked if he'd heard correctly that he'd have to buy the vending machines and, if so, how much would they cost him. Robby explained that Vendor Opportunity Unlimited wanted its distributors to demonstrate their "commitment" by participating financially, paying "wholesale prices for state-of-the-art vending machines." Vend-Op had found, he explained, that its distributors maintained and stocked the machines more conscientiously (and profitably) if they owned them. In regard to price, the machines cost "just" $2,999 each, with a ten percent discount with the purchase of ten or more. With profits averaging $150 per machine per week, they'd be paid for in "just a few months," enthused Robby. "After that, it's nothing but gravy for the distributor." Robby reminded Vernon that Vend-Op would install his vending machines in "choice locations guaranteed to yield high profits."

Vernon had enough presence of mind to ask Robby how Vend-Op made money selling machines at wholesale prices while also providing training and location services. Praising Vernon as an "astute businessman," Robby explained that Vend-Op was among the largest purchasers of candy in America, commanding unbeatable discounts from manufacturers. Vend-Op then sold the candy and snacks in bulk to its distributors at wholesale prices, which included a reasonable mark-up for the company. "Vend-Op profits on the candy sold by its distributors," said Robby. "Vend-Op believes in partnership. The company makes money only if its distributors make money."

The next day, an overnight courier service hand-delivered a friendly note from Robby Jones along with a color brochure full of photos, equipment specifications, and rapturous testimonials from people who'd gotten rich after becoming authorized distributors for Vendor Opportunity Unlimited. Vernon read the materials with interest. Without discussing it with his wife, he completed the short application form, overstating the money he actually had available for investment as $75,000, thinking a higher sum would improve his chances. Though uncertain about partnering with Vend-Op, Vernon certainly enjoyed considering it; he felt light-headed with entrepreneurial excitement, imagining how his nest egg might grow into something substantial, how he might soon be smiling like those lucky distributors pictured in the brochure.

Just four days later, Robby Jones called Vernon with exciting news: the selection committee had agreed to offer him a distributorship, starting with fifteen vending machines with an option on ten more if he demonstrated managerial competence. "The committee wavered a bit but I told them you'd be great," gushed Robby. "I'll send you the agreement and some other papers for you to sign today. Get them back to me immediately, before someone else from your area gets considered, or you may lose out." Robby then explained the terms of the deal. Vernon would invest $44,784.50 (payable in advance), itemized as follows: $40,486.50 for the vending machines, $1,299 for shipping, and $2,999 in bulk product (candy, chips, pretzels, and other popular snacks). His distributorship locations would be confirmed and his machines and supplies would be shipped after receipt of his payment.

Though he'd liked fantasizing about becoming a vending tycoon, the real prospect of actually parting with his savings caused Vernon to waver, particularly without first discussing it with his wife. This was something he dreaded doing. With little experience making weighty decisions, Vernon had yet to learn one of the cardinal rules of invest-ment, which is that it's always a bad deal if you're nervous telling your spouse about it beforehand. Robby sensed Vernon's doubts and tried to lessen them by providing the name and phone number of a Vend-Op distributor who'd done very well in a very short time with just fifteen machines. Vernon agreed to call the man, saying he'd make his decision after talking to him. The very next day, the Vend-Op ref-erence called Vernon, who'd been procrastinating about placing the call himself, paralyzed by the prospect of embracing a possibility (a vending distributorship) and facing a certainty (a skeptical wife). The caller told Vernon how he'd become fat and happy with his Vend-Op distributorship—happy from all the profits and fat from all the candy and snacks he'd been eating. (Of course, only later did it occur to Ver-non that legitimate references usually wait to be called, rather than making the call themselves.)

Gripped by entrepreneurial zeal and mounting certitude, Vernon Yost pondered the relative merits of telling his wife before or after making the deal, and unfortunately he settled on telling her after.

Angelina Yost had absolutely no head for business, he reasoned, and a full disclosure of his plans would surely lead to an argument. When it came to their savings, Angelina was like the squirrel who'd rather starve before consuming its store of nuts in order to avoid running short someday. Vernon saw himself as like the farmer who'd rather plant those nuts and have bountiful harvests in the future. In short, they were philosophically opposed in regard to money. The next day, Vernon sent the signed agreements to Vend-Op, along with the biggest check he'd ever written in his life. He never bothered to consult with an attorney, fearful that any further delay might cause Vend-Op to rescind its offer.

Vernon was still thinking about the best way to tell his wife about Vend-Op when a truck pulled up to deliver all fifteen vending machines and about forty large boxes of candy and snacks. This sent Angelina into a fit that lasted (according to Vernon's later reckoning) just shy of two years. Needless to say, Vernon felt some urgency to get the machines out of their garage and into their profit-making locations just as quickly as possible. He called Robby Jones (his sole contact at Vend-Op) to get things moving along. Robby referred him to "Mike Smith," who'd been assigned the job of finding locations for Vernon's machines. Unfortunately, Mike was always (according to his recording) away from his desk and never bothered to respond to Vernon's many voice messages.

Vernon started worrying in earnest after unpacking one of the vending machines, an inferior-looking product that had looked much more impressive in the promotional photographs. Made from flimsy sheet metal, the entire machine would twist and torque and make weird metallic wow-wow-wow noises whenever moved or lifted. After some coaxing by Vernon, Angelina nervously inspected his sure-fire, money-making mechanical means to riches. This triggered a crying spell so intense it induced a minor asthma attack.

About a week after that unfortunate incident, Vernon received written notification that Vendor Opportunity Unlimited had arranged for "one or more" of Vernon's vending machines to be placed at a "truck stop" about twenty miles outside of the city. Deciding it would be prudent to reconnoiter before renting a van, Vernon immediately drove out to see the place. To his dismay, Vernon discovered the "truck stop" was actually an old service station along a minor route, its automotive bays converted into a cheesy snack room with about ten unimpressive vending machines already located there, several stocked with exactly the same snacks Vernon had on hand for his machines. There wasn't a soul in the place other than the owner, who disclosed that he'd received fifty dollars "consideration" from Vend-Op. In return, he'd agreed to accept at least one of Vernon's vending machines, though the profit split still had to be negotiated. Stunned by what he'd learned, Vernon drove home in a daze, fully aware at last that he'd been snookered.

Investigation and Aftermath

Determined to minimize his losses, Vernon called Vend-Op to arrange for the return of the machines and demand a full refund under the company's "no questions asked, money back guarantee." Vernon fully expected to forfeit all of the shipping costs, which he saw as the price he'd have to pay for a valuable lesson—some people just aren't to be trusted. Noticeably less friendly to him now, Robby Jones made a half-hearted attempt to talk him out of returning the vending machines, but Vernon wouldn't hear of it. Robby promised to have the "return department" mail him the necessary "shipping labels" to ensure he'd be properly credited. Of course, Vernon never received those shipping labels.

About ten days later, Vernon told his anguished story to Daniel Hudson, a capable and empathetic attorney. Before he'd even finished hearing it all, Daniel concluded that Vernon had been scammed and that hiring an attorney would be the equivalent of pouring money down a rat-hole. He felt like the family doctor who had to deliver the painful news that there was no hope of recovery. Daniel gently pointed out that Vend-Op was a corporation in an entirely different jurisdiction; that the agreement had to be interpreted (and litigated) under the laws of a state over a thousand miles away; that the cost of litigation would be considerable; that the written agreement heavily favored Vend-Op, and that any successful judgment (however un-likely) against the company would probably be uncollectible. Daniel concluded by candidly telling Vernon to sell the machines himself and chalk up his losses to experience.

Vernon insisted on engaging Daniel nonetheless, not because he hadn't been listening (he had been), but because he so greatly feared telling Angelina what the lawyer had said. Paying a retainer was less agonizing than being justly attacked by an anxious spouse who'd already concluded the worst about her husband's poor judgment. Like so many culpable husbands in his situation, Vernon preferred touting false hope to acknowledging the grim truth. Daniel Hudson reluctantly accepted a $500 retainer, knowing that if he declined to represent Vernon, some other, more mercenary lawyer would just charge him more. Daniel called in an old friend, an investigator who'd collaborated with him on many cases. Splitting the retainer, the two agreed to develop information they expected would discourage Vernon from throwing good money after bad. In essence, the two profes-sionals looked upon Vernon as something like a charity case worthy of pro bono work.

The investigator started digging into Vendor Opportunity Un-limited and the people behind it. His findings came as no surprise to Daniel Hudson. Vendor Opportunity Unlimited (aka Vend-Op) was a newly formed corporation, less than three months old when Vernon first learned of it, owned by an ex-convict named Lawrence "Lucky" Fulcrum, who'd been associated with scores of failed corporations. The attorney general's office from the state where it was incorporated had received numerous complaints over the years from consumers and franchisees regarding Lucky Fulcrum's business practices, in-cluding a few recent ones already concerning Vend-Op. The Federal Trade Commission, according to the helpful assistant attorney gen-eral, had also received complaints about Fulcrum's companies, which had repeatedly violated the FTC's "franchise rule" by failing to pro-vide legally required disclosures before entering into binding agree-ments. The assistant AG characterized Fulcrum as a "low-life scam artist" who protected himself with carefully drafted agreements and sham contract fulfillment (sending shoddy products and providing other bogus services) that made a criminal investigation and possible indictment a "non-starter." Other than logging a complaint, the FTC would undoubtedly do nothing, either. Vernon's problems with Vend-Op were a civil matter, requiring resolution in a civil court of law like any other contractual business dispute.

Vendor Opportunity Unlimited went out of business less than a week later, a fact confirmed by its disconnected telephone lines. The investigator had planned to pose as an interested prospect and tape the misrepresentations of "Robby Jones," undoubtedly a fictitious name for an abettor in Lucky Fulcrum's scheme. The investigator traced the business to an old warehouse subdivided into spaces occupied by marginal companies, most of which would likely fail within a year. Over the telephone, the building owner fumed that Vend-Op had moved out owing him three month's rent, which he knew he'd never collect. In other words, Vernon had plenty of company among those who'd been ripped-off by Vendor Opportunity Unlimited. Even the telephone company got stiffed.

Vernon Yost sold his fifteen vending machines for $200 each to a local college, which placed them in undergraduate dorms. Vernon actually felt fortunate receiving that much for them after the investigator pointed out that an internet dealer was offering the same machines refurbished for $99 plus shipping. Vernon heard some months later that several of the machines he'd sold had been smashed, presumably by students frustrated when snacks hadn't been properly dispensed after money had been inserted. Two other machines had simply disappeared in the dead of night.

Angelina eventually forgave her husband, recognizing that his many virtues far outweighed his shortcomings as an investor. Vernon became a much sought-after handyman, fixing everything from sprinkler systems to electrical wiring for his gratified neighbors. The neighborhood children still talk about the Halloween when Vernon dressed up as SpongeBob SquarePants. Every trick-or-treater that year received great handfuls of goodies from SpongeBob, who generously gave away forty boxes of candy and snacks in the course of one very special night.

□ □ □ **CASE #2—FERRIS DUNKEL:**
"LAST YEAR'S ASSET, THIS YEAR'S LIABILITY"

Ferris Dunkel was an ordinary guy, hard working and dependable, who hated his job as a dispatcher for a trucking company. In truth, it wasn't the work that Ferris hated, it was his boss—a nasty type who enjoyed maltreating employees simply for the fun of it, daily satisfying his twisted need to intimidate others.

For six years Ferris dreamed of quitting—telling his boss to shove it, and becoming his own boss—a hopeful dream that helped Ferris get through many a bad day. His chance to make his dream a reality came when his elderly father passed away, leaving an estate valued at $480,000 that was split between Ferris and his sister. Rather than squandering this windfall, Ferris planned to invest the money in an established business, knowing he'd otherwise dribble it away on sports cars, fast boats, and other frivolous things he temperamentally found so irresistible. Though he coveted expensive flashy toys, he coveted his freedom even more. The toys, he reasoned, would come later.

Unfortunately, Ferris could not decide where he should invest his inheritance. He considered buying a neighborhood bar, but worried that he'd become a sodden alcoholic with a spongy liver. He thought about buying a local motorcycle dealership, but worried about the shaggy clientele smelling of leather and cigarettes. He considered buying an old-fashioned ice cream parlor, but worried he'd grow obscenely obese with a serious cholesterol problem. The more perplexed he became, the more pressured he felt to choose something, anything, that would free him from the oppressive job that sapped his self-respect.

When Ferris learned, however, that Ice Kingdom Inc. might be available, he knew at once he had to buy it. As a child, Ferris had loved accompanying his father to Ice Kingdom, the local ice manufacturing plant, to buy those great blocks of ice for the family picnics each summer. Nostalgic memories of those happy times would accompany Ferris as an adult whenever he stopped to purchase cubed or block ice. He fondly remembered his father indulging his awkward attempts to wrestle the massive, slippery blocks into the trunk of the family sedan. At just the critical moment, his bemused father would always step up and help him drop it in with a thud, the car springs briefly sagging under the frozen mass. In hindsight, those childhood ice blocks were like frozen hourglasses, tracking the passage of hot summer days drip by happy drip. Ferris Dunkel sorely missed his dad, but he felt his reassuring presence that fateful summer day when he walked into Ice Kingdom for a bag of ice and walked out planning to buy the business.

Doby Stockler, the son of the man who'd started the business, had owned and operated Ice Kingdom for the last thirteen years. Lacking his father's ardent dedication, Doby attended his customers as if slowly dying from ennui. He'd known Ferris for many years, not well of course but as a long-standing customer who'd linger after a purchase, a true Ice Kingdom loyalist. "Know anyone who'd want to buy this place?" asked Doby, lugging a bag of ice from the freezer, looking haggard and exhausted.

"I might be interested," answered Ferris nonchalantly, inwardly stunned that Heaven would present this opportunity in his hour of need.

No other customers were in the place at the time, so the two started talking. Doby admitted that his being burnt out was his reason for selling, along with his needing a change. Ferris could relate. Doby then gave him a complete tour of the plant, talked about its production capacity, and outlined the financials in general terms. The business owned the building and all the equipment, had no debt, and yielded about $80,000 in net income after expenses. Ice Kingdom employed only two other people in addition to Doby, one who helped with sales and production and another who delivered ice to its various commercial accounts. Doby described the equipment as "old but working" and the delivery truck as "OK," though it had almost 200,000 miles on its odometer.

Ferris played it cool and did not betray his excitement at the prospect of owning a business he'd long associated with happy times from his past. With a handshake, the two agreed to have further discussions to explore the possibility of deal. They met at length again the very next day and Doby told Ferris he wanted $400,000 for the business and real estate, which he called a bargain considering that a new plant with comparable capacity would cost as much as three times that figure. Ferris shook his head and said $400,000 was more than he wanted to invest in a business, shrewdly hoping to dicker. Ferris soon had him down to $350,000, with $250,000 payable at closing and $100,000 payable over time, financed by Doby and secured with a first mortgage on the real estate and equipment.

A cautious man, Ferris called his attorney and his accountant to get them involved in the process to make sure everything was above-board and transferred properly. He asked his accountant to spend time at Ice Kingdom and carefully examine all the financial records, to confirm that the business had generated the gross profits represented by Doby. Ferris figured about $150,000 of the purchase price could be allocated to the real estate and about $200,000 could be allocated to the actual business yielding about $80,000 per year. Any business that sells for two and a half times earnings, he reckoned, would be a very good deal. After spending two days checking the books, Ferris's accountant came back with encouraging news. Ice Kingdom had had remarkably stable earnings for many years. If anything, the accountant noted, the historic earnings could be enhanced with tax breaks for depreciation and interest payments. Then, bestowing the ultimate blessing for a professional adviser, his accountant commented that he'd be willing to invest if Ferris wanted to carve out a minority interest.

Actually, Ferris already had someone in mind as a possible minority partner: his younger sister. His father's bequest had made this fabulous opportunity possible, so it seemed only fitting that he offer his sister part of the action. After his accountant gave the business an enthusiastic thumbs-up, Ferris met with his sister and easily persuaded her to invest $50,000 for 20 percent of the business. As manager, Ferris agreed to draw just $50,000 per year in salary, and all profits above that would be split 80/20 between them. Including his sister in the deal would also leave Ferris approximately $40,000 from his father's bequest, enough to buy just one new toy: an impeccably restored 1970 Corvette Stingray he'd recently seen in a local dealer's showroom. He secretly imagined that this splendid car parked in front of the Ice Kingdom might actually draw in new customers. Ferris was too fiscally conservative, however, to count on any increased patronage until he actually saw it.

Ten days later, Ferris was the very proud owner of his own business. His attorney had reviewed and approved the legal documents transferring the corporation and its assets to Ferris and his sister. The documents contained no representations and warranties other than those regarding clear title, much like those found in a real estate transaction. Ferris acknowledged in writing that he was buying all assets and equipment in "as is" condition. The same day the deal closed, Ferris impulsively went out and bought the Corvette and drove it home, hollering for all the world to hear, "Free at last . . . free at last . . . thank God I'm free at last!"

Aftermath

When he submitted his resignation to his ill-tempered boss, Ferris found himself incapable of telling him off despite the years of verbal abuse he'd endured. In hindsight, Ferris was very glad he hadn't spoken out, considering the way things ultimately turned out. Bouncing with happiness and excitement, Ferris breathlessly told his boss about how he had purchased Ice Kingdom and invited him to stop by sometime. "Your first block of ice will be complimentary," offered Ferris generously.

Ferris' first day as owner of Ice Kingdom was truly a happy one. Doby agreed to stick around for a day or two to make sure Ferris understood "the quirks," as Doby called them, of the ice manufacturing equipment. He explained how the compressors were old and temperamental and required constant attention. Ferris noticed for the first time the odd discordant noises coming from the massive compressors and the strange electrical smells also being emitted.

Though he'd met the two employees before, Ferris hadn't wanted them to know he was buying the business, concerned that if the word got out someone else would try to buy the business, potentially driving up the price or, even worse, snaking it away from him entirely. Therefore, when Doby introduced Ferris as the "new owner" to Joseph, a longtime Ice Kingdom employee, the man simply gaped at him. Ferris interpreted his silence as surprise. In fact, Joseph had stared at Ferris with mute incredulity, astonished anyone could be so stupid as to buy a business with so many serious problems. Scott, the delivery truck driver, seemed similarly stunned to learn that Ferris would henceforth be his boss. Of course, Joseph and Scott eventually spoke up, but by then it was too late for Ferris. The last thing Doby did before leaving on a long vacation was to slip Ferris the business card of Philip Smirnoff, a repair technician specializing in refrigeration equipment. "Philip knows all about the compressors," he said cryptically. "He might be able to help if something goes wrong."

Things did go wrong with the compressors soon thereafter, but that was only the beginning. When one compressor stopped working entirely, Ferris pulled out Philip Smirnoff's business card and called him. After identifying himself as Ice Kingdom's new owner, Ferris told Philip about the downed compressor. "So one finally gave up the ghost," said Philip with a chuckle. "I'm amazed it took so long." Philip arrived later that morning to examine the mechanical corpse and officially declared it dead with no hope of resurrection. He also told Ferris that the other compressor was also near the end and should be replaced. "Didn't that pirate Stockler tell you the equipment was shot?" he asked.

While Ferris was calling around the next day for used compressors (new ones were prohibitively expensive), Ice Kingdom was served with a lawsuit. A notorious serial litigant from the area claimed he'd been sickened some months earlier by ice contaminated with salmonella bacteria, causing him lingering gastrointestinal problems. The lawsuit sought compensation for indeterminate financial damages for medical bills and physical incapacity. Having never been sued before, Ferris nearly choked from apprehension reading the complaint and asked Joseph if he knew anything about the aggrieved party and his allegations. "So that crazy codger actually went through with it," said Joseph, shaking his head. He then told Ferris how the complainant had been badgering them for months, claiming that Ice Kingdom had "poisoned" him and vowing to sue if he didn't get his "just recompense."

Just weeks before Ferris bought the company, Joseph explained, Doby got into a shouting match with the man and had to call the cops when the man wouldn't leave the premises.

Two days after that drama, according to Joseph, the city health department descended on Ice Kingdom. Apparently the aggrieved man, then on a vendetta, had identified Ice Kingdom's ice cubes as the likely source of his Salmonella poisoning, triggering an expedited inspection. The health inspectors failed to find any evidence of the pathogen, though Ice Kingdom was cited for multiple code violations, which required costly physical upgrades to improve production sanitation. Joseph expressed surprise that Doby Stockler hadn't disclosed this important information.

After that, things went from bad to worse. The delivery truck's transmission finally gave out, something Scott had been expecting for months. The renewal of the company's insurance policy would almost double its cost. The water and electricity rates were going up. One of the key commercial accounts, a wholesale fish jobber, filed for bankruptcy protection owing $3,000 to Ice Kingdom, which, as an unsecured creditor, had no hope of ever getting paid. Two grocery store chains and about a dozen convenient food marts dropped Ice Kingdom, switching to a supplier that had just opened a new ice plant nearby, providing a better product for less money. In fact, this new competitor quickly drove the stake through the economic heart of Ice Kingdom, and Ferris eventually concluded that further investment in the business made little sense.

Unfortunately, before reaching that conclusion, Ferris had sunk additional money into improvements, borrowing against his Corvette and nicking his sister for a $5,000 loan to the corporation. When he'd exhausted all of his own financial resources and his sister refused him any further loans, Ferris disconsolately recognized he might lose the business, which was hemorrhaging money and still required several more expensive upgrades. Ferris tried unsuccessfully for some months to bring in new investors, and though a few did examine the business, they quickly passed. They rightly concluded that Ice Kingdom would have a tough time surviving with rising operating costs, declining sales, and the formidable competition from the new ice plant across town.

A year after he'd purchased Ice Kingdom, Ferris Dunkel found himself back at work with the trucking company he'd been so eager to escape. After Ferris defaulted on the mortgage, Doby Stockler repossessed the place and sold off all its salvageable fixtures. He then demolished the building and constructed a profitable self-storage facility in its place. Ferris lost his entire investment along with the money his sister had in the business, sadly straining what had been a very close relationship. He also lost his beloved Corvette, which, by his own admission, was even more painful than losing the business.

□ □ □ CASE #3—WILLIAM JOHNSON:
"DEEP POCKETS, EMPTY PROMISES"

Sixty-five-year-old William Johnson chose a family reunion over Thanksgiving dinner as the most fitting time to tell his two daughters that he'd decided to sell the family business. Both children lived out of state, one married to an orthopedic surgeon in California and the other single and an accomplished graphic artist in New York City. A sentimental man, William shared the momentous news by proposing a toast: "To a prosperous and carefree future without burdens of work."

Over the previous thirty years, William had painstakingly built his company into a solid and steady performer, always providing a good living for his family. As was the case with so many entrepreneurs, the bulk of William's net worth was tied up in his business, a small distribution company dealing in various items used in the automotive industry. The company's yearly sales were just under $5 million, from which William netted approximately $290,000 per year in salary, benefits, and dividends. The company had no debt and owned about $750,000 in tangible assets, all fully depreciated for tax purposes, mostly vehicles and office paraphernalia.

William embraced his wife Mildred and their daughters in a celebratory group hug that lasted about a minute. William told his daughters that he and their mom wanted to travel more, particularly to visit their grandchildren in California. Over pumpkin pie and coffee, he told everyone he hoped to net $2 million, a reasonable sum considering the business could be capably run with existing management. The marketing director, Bobby Holcomb, and the treasurer, Mary Katherine Bingham, had been with the firm for more than a decade. Both were tireless and responsible employees, entirely capable of managing the business without him.

William told his family he'd been negotiating with someone named Kyle Hartington, a wealthy newcomer to the area who'd created a stir among the social elite after contributing a generous sum at a recent hospital fundraiser. By chance at that event, William had met Hartington, a suave middle-aged gentleman, well mannered and impeccably dressed, who had the air of someone who came from privilege and old money. Of course, chance—the guileless attendant of fate—can alter a person's future, but not always for the better. While waiting patiently in line at the open bar, William had sociably introduced himself to Kyle. The two began talking, a conversation that led to their sitting together during dinner. William would later wish he'd skipped that second glass of white wine and sat instead with old friends and cronies.

At dinner, William asked Kyle about himself and what had brought him to the area. Kyle explained that his wife Joyce, a lovely woman seated on the other side of him, had grown up in the area and had wanted to return. Kyle told him that as a "mostly passive" investor, he could manage his company portfolio from almost anywhere. He said he owned controlling interests in about a half-dozen small companies back East that pretty much ran themselves. William quipped that Kyle should consider buying his business, more as a way to talk about his own accomplishments than as an authentic overture to bargain. Kyle looked at William with interest. "Tell me about your business," he'd said. "I'm always looking for new opportunities."

Over the following weeks, William met with Kyle several times for lunch and warmed to the idea of selling his company. Without being too forward, Kyle expressed interest and casually asked about a variety of related subjects, subtly conducting his due-diligence in a proper and dignified manner. William enjoyed conversing with such a knowledgeable and experienced businessman, something he rarely got to do. At home, he and Mildred almost never talked business, a touchy subject that when broached too often left each feeling sour and underappreciated. After one particularly engaging luncheon conversation, Kyle asked William if he were truly interested in selling his business, yes or no. "If you're just flirting with me," said Kyle with a wry smile, "I'd like to know. After all, even ardent suitors will lose interest if there isn't any chance for consummation." William laughed and said he'd be willing to sell, contingent of course upon price and a few other issues.

Given the green light, Kyle engaged his lawyers and financial advisors, who began digging deeply into the company's assets, operations, and finances, a process that thoroughly unnerved William. He worried that his employees, vendors, and customers might become uneasy, and possibly upset, if they heard of the pending sale. William wondered how they'd react if the deal fell through; would there be residual distrust that could hurt his business? To show good faith, Kyle and William signed a nonbinding "letter of intent" which outlined the general terms of the deal subject to further examination. William felt much more relaxed thereafter, because Kyle agreed to his $2 million asking price after verifying the company's assets and profitability over the previous five years.

The snag in the transaction occurred when Kyle asked William to finance the deal, offering $300,000 down with the $1.7 million balance payable in a year, with interest accruing at two points above the prime interest rate. Kyle's request surprised William, who'd made it abundantly clear that he wanted to be cashed out, a provision even addressed in the letter of intent. William bluntly told Kyle to speak with his banker if he needed financing. Kyle responded by saying he had other, larger deals pending that had somewhat cooled his enthusiasm for the deal with William. Those other opportunities, he said, required his remaining financially liquid for the near term.

To reassure William, Kyle offered to disclose (on a strictly confidential basis) his updated financial statement along with his tax returns for the previous three years. Kyle also voiced his concern in regard to William's knee-jerk refusal to provide short-term financing, causing him to question the underlying value of the business. Kyle pointed out that the $1.7 million would be fully secured with the company's assets. "Certainly you have confidence in your business," said Kyle calmly, adding, "but if you don't, then I shouldn't either." On a more conciliatory note, Kyle told William he wouldn't be offended in the slightest if William changed his mind about selling.

William spent the night tossing and turning, aggravated by this last-minute demand. He didn't need the money right away, however, which helped him accede to Kyle's request. Though his wife thought him overly cautious, William did ask to see Kyle's tax returns and current financial statement. He also called Kyle's financial adviser, who confirmed that Kyle had about $14 million in net worth and $3.2 million in taxable earnings the previous year.

At his lawyer's suggestion, William asked Kyle to personally guarantee the $1.7 million note. Kyle refused, saying his even asking made him question, once again, William's confidence in the value of his company. "I haven't asked you to guarantee the future profitability of your company," he countered coolly. William backed off and the attorneys completed the purchase agreement. Closing occurred some weeks later. William felt comforted knowing the $1.7 million note was just for a year. What could possibly go wrong in a year, particularly with Bobby Holcomb and Mary Katherine Bingham capably running the company?

Two weeks after closing, William got a call from Mary Katherine, who'd tracked him down in California while he was visiting his daughter's family. To William's astonishment, Mary Katherine told him that Hartington had just fired her as company treasurer. She tearfully told him that Kyle had said simply that he wanted his "own man," someone he could trust, to monitor his investment. William promised to call Kyle to try to get her reinstated immediately. After hanging up the phone, William sat by himself for awhile feeling shaken and bewildered. A pit grew in his stomach, a gnawing visceral indicator that something was seriously wrong.

Investigation and Aftermath

William initially had trouble reaching Hartington, who didn't return his phone calls. When he finally caught him at home several days later, Kyle stubbornly refused even to consider reinstating Mary Katherine—in fact, he refused even to talk about it. He told William he wanted his own man to protect not only his investment but also William's sizable security interest in the company, a comment that William took more as a threat than a comfort. Kyle told him that the new treasurer, a man named Dominick Luigosi, had worked for him in the past; he was a proficient manager who would ensure the future success of his company. Kyle warned William not to make trouble and cited the "noninterference" provision in the purchase agreement along with the clauses conveying control to the purchaser. William later studied the agreement very carefully (something he realized he should have done before) and learned to his chagrin that he had little recourse, save repossessing the company if Kyle failed to pay the $1.7 million due in eleven months.

William felt terrible calling Mary Katherine and telling her his hands were contractually tied. She angrily accused him of "conspiring" with Kyle and, as a member of a protected class, vowed to sue the company for age discrimination and unlawful discharge. With a heavy heart, William listened as she denounced him for failing her after years of exemplary service, leaving her to twist in the wind after he had cashed out. What could he say? He had failed her. He should have protected her contractually, but he hadn't even thought about it during his negotiations with Hartington. He naively thought her position secure based on her competence and her thorough knowledge of the business. True to her word, Mary Katherine filed a lawsuit against the company about a week later.

In the weeks that followed, Kyle couldn't meet or even find time to talk with William, conveying messages through his "scheduler" that he was unavailable, out-of-town, previously committed and other such excuses. Increasingly worried, William called Bobby Holcomb, the company's marketing director, and the two met later that day at a quiet restaurant. Bobby told William that Dominick Luigosi, under his authority as executive vice president and treasurer, had raised product prices 6 percent across the board, causing discontent and some defections among their customers. Bobby was completely in the dark concerning Hartington's future plans, though he'd heard a rumor that the company had been put up for sale, the likely explanation for all of the "suits" who'd been parading through the office recently. Bobby also told William that Luigosi seemed a "shady character" who was furtive and unfriendly with everyone.

Incapable of sitting still, William met with his attorney who had nothing comforting to tell him. He reminded William that he'd pushed for personal guarantees on Kyle's note, which took William somewhat aback. William's main concern had been for his former employees and recent happenings at the company. He'd always assumed he'd get his money. Obviously his attorney, given recent events, wasn't quite so sure. After further conversation, William's attorney agreed to engage an investigator to find out if Kyle Hartington was trying to unload the company and, if so, on what terms.

About a week later, the investigator reported back with disturbing information. Hartington had indeed been trying to sell the company for $2.5 million dollars, a substantial markup from the $2 million purchase price for which he'd acquired it just two months earlier. The investigator's more alarming news was that Hartington had a history of "flipping" and "bleed-outs." Apparently, Kyle had made much of his money by buying small companies, almost always financed by the sellers, and then flipping (selling) them quickly for a tidy profit. He also had a history of siphoning money from those he could not easily flip ("bleeding them out") and then defaulting on the notes, thus rarely suffering losses on his deals. The prior owners would be forced to take their businesses back, drained of cash and burdened with new operating debts.

Hampered by privacy laws, the investigator could not say for sure that Hartington had been draining money from William's former company, but thought it a reasonable assumption. Dominick Luigosi had been Hartington's operative in previous bleed-outs and even a few "bust-outs"—cases where the acquired companies had been so financially depleted that they eventually failed after Hartington walked away. The investigator also had learned that Hartington had been sued many times for his business dealings, but that he'd almost always escaped serious consequences, protected by contracts validated by the courts. Kyle Hartington's reputation in his prior hometown was so abysmal that he'd become a social outcast, which was probably the real reason he'd moved away.

In business, the painful truth is always preferable to blissful ignorance. Though William did not like what he'd learned about Kyle Hartington, he could at least act on the information. With impressive energy and tenacity, William took legal steps to protect his security interest. Empowered by a sympathetic judge persuaded by his lawyer's effective pleadings, William was able to monitor the company's finances, which probably prevented Hartington from wrecking the company completely. Kyle's draws from the company, for example, were limited by the court to an amount equal to William's salary and dividends from the prior year. Of course, William found it galling that Kyle got paid anything considering that he did nothing but screw up the company's balance sheet. During that entire dreadful year, William worked tirelessly as a defender of his former employees, customers, and suppliers, looking out for their interests as well as his own. Not surprisingly, Hartington failed to sell the company for $2.5 million, and he and also failed to pay the $1.7 million owed William. William ended up taking back the company, which was damaged but repairable, and immediately rehired Mary Katherine Bingham, who he repaid half of her lost wages and all of her legal expenses to settle her lawsuit still pending in the Court of Common Pleas.

It took almost three years for William to bring his company back to where it had been financially before Hartington's acquisition. Now seventy years old, William plans to sell his company and retire sometime soon, but vows to handle the transaction more cautiously. For starters, he intends to check out every prospective purchaser thoroughly before beginning negotiations.

□ □ □ **COMMENTARY AND ANALYSIS**

Second only to owning a home, Americans dream of owning a successful business. Every year, millions of optimistic dreamers, alone or in partnership, either start a new business or buy an existing one. Most of them will either fail or see their investment returns falling well short of expectations. Despite the likelihood of disappointment, starry-eyed entrepreneurs always expect to beat the odds and prosper. In fact, entrepreneurs never expect to fail. For most of them, failure is not even a possibility, let alone a probability.

As an investigator accustomed to observing the consequences of deals gone bad, I believe that optimism is usually nothing more than wishful thinking, a form of self-delusion more likely to precipitate wrenching failure than cheery success. I also believe that cautious skepticism—which entails accepting and facing the possibility of failure in any business deal—ironically improves one's chances for success. In truth, most business startups and acquisitions have major flaws, some even fatal, and identifying them should be the first priority when making any deal. Such skepticism is the cornerstone when it comes to managing investment risk.

In each of the preceding cases, the three unfortunate dupes— William, Vernon, and Ferris—failed to uncover easily discoverable information that, had they known it beforehand, would have kept them from entering into the deals that ended up costing them so much. Each eventually got fully and painfully educated, but only after it was too late to avoid getting burned. In certain respects, these three represent the rule, not the exception, in business today. Most businesspeople don't do a good job of evaluating deals before plunging into them. More often than not, their due diligence is cursory and inadequate, the equivalent of kicking the tires when buying a used auto.

Due diligence in acquisitions is the investigative process of identifying a target business's assets, liabilities (present and contingent), contractual obligations, reputation, regulatory compliance, financial standing, ownership, competition, and all of the other vital factors that may affect the present value and future viability of the enterprise. Essentially a homework exercise, due diligence generally requires input from a multidisciplinary team galvanized by the time-honored admonition of *caveat emptor,* or buyer beware. In other words, investors have the obligation to look out for themselves. Let's look back at the three preceding cases, starting with the most experienced business-man and the problems he faced.

William Johnson case

William Johnson, of course, learned the hard way that the *caveat emptor* principle should be extended to sellers as well as buyers. A consummate manipulator, Kyle Hartington seduced William with his money and social polish, luring him into a trusting business relation-ship based on assumptions William made about Kyle's integrity. In fact, personal net worth should never be mistaken for personal worth. From my experience, significant wealth should often prompt caution, not comfort, particularly when that wealth is shamelessly flaunted by a dealmaker. Over the years, I have seen many cases where people like Kyle shared eye-popping financial statements on a "confidential basis" in order to overcome legitimate concerns or business hesitancy. Those bestowed the confidence often ended up losing their shirts. Culturally, most Americans are secretive about their personal net worth. Those who aren't should always be viewed carefully; in many cases, they should probably be avoided altogether.

How should William have determined if Kyle was a responsible investor with the integrity to go with his financial means? He should have gotten to know him better by carefully probing his past. Selling a closely held business is always a stressful experience for its owner, akin to an intense but uncertain courtship marked by soaring hopes and destabilizing anxieties. According to the unwritten rules of ro-mance, the pursued is prudent to wait before becoming too intimate with an eager suitor. Similarly, business owners should always confirm that a prospective purchaser (or partner) is true and worthy before getting too involved. William should have questioned Kyle carefully about himself and his business background, not tactlessly but in an inquisitive and nonthreatening manner, to probe for specifics about his career and prior business relationships. For example, William could have used the "reluctant spouse" pretext, requesting a detailed curriculum vitae from Kyle to help persuade his wife that Kyle was just the man to preserve and nurture their precious family business.

By reconstructing Kyle's business history, William easily could have identified people who'd had firsthand business experience dealing with Kyle. William could then have sought out some of these individuals, preferably those who'd had similar transactions with Kyle, and spoken with them. Even more importantly, William should have conducted a thorough litigation search in every jurisdiction where Kyle had ever lived or operated a business. This would have entailed checking courthouse indexes for Kyle's name and the names of the enterprises with which he'd been associated. This is precisely what his attorney's investigator did for William, unfortunately well after any findings could have helped him. The court records, of course, demonstrated that Kyle was an unscrupulous opportunist interested only in squeezing quick cash from his investments, shamelessly hurting others in the process. Had he learned this earlier, William would never have entrusted or conveyed his business—in essence, his life's work—to Kyle Hartington. Even if Kyle had doubled his offer and agreed to pay cash, William Johnson would never have sold his "child" to someone so contemptible.

Ferris Dunkel case

All too often, investors think they've carefully evaluated an opportunity, when in reality they've hardly begun a proper examination before the deal closes. Ferris Dunkel thought he'd done everything right by engaging his accountant and lawyer to help him with the purchase of Ice Kingdom. His accountant quite correctly confirmed the historical and current earnings of the business. Comforted by his positive analysis, Ferris made the common mistake of using past earnings as a sure predictor of future performance. A business, however, should not be valued on what it has made in the past, but on what it can make in the future. Ferris spent almost no time examining those factors that might affect earnings, specifically the changing market (new competition), manufacturing costs (obsolete equipment), and impending liabilities (regulatory issues and potential litigation). In honesty, Ferris didn't have a clue.

Ferris made another common mistake by letting his emotions

influence his approach to the transaction. His desperation to buy a business, any business, to escape his unhappy employment situation led to an impulsive and hurried purchase. Other strong emotions also affected his judgment. Ferris associated Ice Kingdom with happier times, and his nostalgia gave a rosy tint to the prospective deal. Emotions may cause investors subconsciously to neglect or rush proper due diligence, their heartfelt hopes impeding any mindful analysis that might produce results that would undercut the happy dream. People in romantic courtship, temporarily blinded by their hopes and longings, often overlook faults that will later grow large and problematic in marriage. Similarly, investors often show the same weakness when acquiring a business, becoming so enraptured in their pursuit, so swept up by momentum, that they rush into costly deals they later regret. Marriages born of impulse usually don't work out. The same holds true in business. The more investors want to make a deal, and the higher their expectations, the greater the likelihood of loss and disappointment over the long run. A cautious approach with conservative expectations is likely to lead to a better result. Financially and emotionally, it is always better to be surprised by success than disappointed by results that fall well short of lofty expectations.

Ferris Dunkel thought he had the right advisors to help with his deal, but he was wrong. His accountant was a decent number-cruncher, but lacked the wider experience needed in acquisitions. His lawyer was outright incompetent, having failed to craft an agreement that included representations, indemnifications, and warranties that could have protected Ferris from serious loss. A good attorney might have made a world of difference. While there are limits to what lawyers can accomplish, carefully drafted contracts can constrain many risks. Warranties and representations also help deter a seller's lies and nondisclosures, and provide a basis for legal remedies when things go wrong. Had Doby Stockler, Ice Kingdom's seller, balked at including them in the contract, Ferris would have been alerted to hidden problems that needed further investigation.

There are over 1 million practicing attorneys in America today and many add little value to business deals for the fees they charge. Though rarely the sole cause, poor lawyering often plays a part in business failures. Furthermore, legal work is always expensive, irrespective of its quality. Even incompetent attorneys bill hundreds of dollars per hour. Few things in business are more galling than paying exorbitant fees to mediocre lawyers who do a lousy job protecting their client's interests. If excellent legal representation costs roughly the same as poor legal representation, doesn't it make sense to use the best possible attorney for deals of consequence? Before even considering a business startup or acquisition, investors should develop a relationship with an outstanding transactional attorney they can trust. Preferably, the relationship will be so close that the attorney will feel their client's pain if the deal goes bad.

Ferris Dunkel's team of advisers also needed more expertise, including someone who could evaluate Ice Kingdom's production (operations and equipment) and someone who could evaluate its market (customer contracts and competition). To that end, Ferris should have asked Doby to identify Ice Kingdom's professional and service providers so that they might be questioned. If Ferris had hired a qualified engineer to lead an independent inspection, Philip Smirnoff, Ice Kingdom's repairman, would have been called before the deal was made and asked what maintenance and repairs had been done (and what needed to be done) on the ice-manufacturing equipment. Service providers are generally frank and honest about hidden problems, and their insights are often invaluable. In most acquisitions, the buyer is largely dependent on the quality and quantity of the information provided by the seller. The seller typically knows far more about the defects and overall condition of the business, but may not be forthcoming with negative information, as was certainly the case with Doby Stockler. Conducting extensive interviews with the seller's professional advisers (including the seller's accountant) can significantly reduce this risk.

In addition to questioning Smirnoff, Ferris should also have contacted Ice Kingdom's major customers to assess sales stability and possibly identify hidden problems, such as the impending bankruptcy of the wholesale fish jobber. As part of that exercise, Ferris also should have examined market trends and checked out the competition. He easily could have learned about the new competitor and the large in-

crease in local ice-production capacity, facts that did not bode well for
Ice Kingdom's financial future even if its equipment kept working. Inadequate analysis of competitor positioning and recent (or imminent)
changes in the marketplace can be a fatal flaw in business startups
or acquisitions. Inattention to the competition happens all the time,
even in established, publicly traded companies. Ice Kingdom's competitor, on the other hand, clearly did his homework before building
his new ice plant across town. He was well rewarded for his efforts.
Through competitive analysis, he knew that Ice Kingdom had controlled the local market for decades and enjoyed revenues and profits
on a unit basis well above the national average. As the only game in
town, Ice Kingdom could set prices with little concern of losing market share. Ferris's counterpart rightly saw this as an opportunity. The
local marketplace had become accustomed to a relatively high price
for packaged ice, which a new supplier could easily beat and still be
profitable.

Ferris later learned that the new competitor, as part of his due
diligence, had discreetly evaluated Ice Kingdom's physical plant and
production capabilities, accomplished by talking with others (including Ice Kingdom's repairman) and reconnoitering under the pretense
of buying ice. Before investing a dime in a new facility, he correctly
predicted that Ice Kingdom would be financially burdened by operating inefficiencies and equipment obsolescence, which meant it would
go out of business after losing about 40 percent of market share. Ice
Kingdom's competitor thought the process would take a few years,
but was surprised (and delighted) when Ice Kingdom closed less than
a year after the new plant's opening. The new competitor then was in a
position to raise prices and enjoy much greater earnings and profitability. This entrepreneur benefited from systematic and thoughtful
due diligence before investing; Ferris, on the other hand, suffered
from inadequate and rushed due diligence, missing the fatal flaws in
his transaction. From very different perspectives, both could speak
eloquently about the importance of proper due diligence, affirm-
ing that investment evaluation requires investigation, assessment,
analysis, and the astute judgment of future risk and reward.

Vernon Yost case

Contacting present and former accounts is essential to understanding a business and its prospects for success, something particularly true in franchise deals such as the one that ensnared Vernon Yost. Tens of thousands of gullible people, some desperate to supplement their income, fall for get-rich-quick schemes, enticed by advertisements that appear in reputable newspapers and magazines around the country. The vast majority of these "opportunities" have about the same chance as a lottery ticket of ever paying out.

Most "business opportunity" promotions are nothing but scams that take an investor's money up front and fail to deliver on promises. Some of the more common ones involve vending machines, pay phones, medical billings, arcade games, envelope stuffing, and almost all work-at-home ideas. Typically, scam business advertisements convey the impression that the advertiser is offering a job; the actual purpose, however, is to sell shoddy merchandise. The ads will usually refer to an "opening" or a "money-making opportunity," tempting bait for the unemployed and underemployed. When someone interested calls the advertised telephone number, they invariably get connected with a boiler-room operation staffed by skilled hucksters who can make a financial killing closing fewer than one deal in a hundred tries. Their sales pitch generally includes at least some of the following promises: guaranteed income, risk-free investment, inflated profit projections, locator services, specialized training, great deals on merchandise, repurchase plans, money-back guarantees on merchandise, promises of financial independence, and exclusive territories.

Poor Vernon thought he was dealing with a well-established company with hundreds of successful distributors nationwide. Little did he know he was among the first (and last) franchisees of a company that would open and fold within a matter of months. Innocent, trusting people are at greatest risk of falling for such scams; unfortunately, they usually are among those who can least afford it. Vernon was understandably intrigued by the prospect of earning the $1,500 per week mentioned in the advertisement. Of course, he would have benefited knowing that federal law required Vend-Op to disclose in writing the number and percentages of previous franchise purchasers who'd achieved these earnings. Robby Jones referred to "scores" of distributors achieving this threshold, obviously a brazen lie. The promotional brochure sent by Vend-Op included vague claims of "wealth creation" and "financial success." This brochure, however, did not begin to comply with federal laws that require specific and detailed disclosures to prospective investors.

Franchising is an increasingly popular way to start one's own business, and the law provides specific protections to investors considering this route. The Federal Trade Commission's Franchise Rule requires anyone marketing a franchise business to furnish written disclosures providing key information about the opportunity not less than ten business days prior to accepting money or entering into a contract with an investor. At least in principle, the purpose of the Franchise Rule is to protect potential franchisees (those buying a franchise) and help them make a reasoned assessment of the potential risks and benefits of the offering.

Formally entitled "Disclosure Requirements and Prohibitions Concerning Franchising and Business Opportunity Ventures," the Franchise Rule imposes specific obligations on franchisors (those selling a franchise) in regard to the "advertising, offering, licensing, contracting, sale, or other promotion" of a franchise business. Under the Franchise Rule, an offering entity must disclose in writing the nature of its business and it history, its legal structure, its financial balance sheet, its places of operation, the total number of franchises, the number of franchises terminated or not renewed, the identities and business experience of the principals affiliated with the entity, the litigation history of the entity and its principals, the prior associations of its principals with insolvent or bankrupt companies, an itemization of what will be provided, all fees to be paid, and other applicable information concerning training, exclusive territories, and other seller and buyer responsibilities. Had Vendor Opportunity Unlimited complied with its disclosure obligations under the Franchise Rule, even someone as inexperienced and gullible as Vernon would have shied away from the deal.

Of course, scammers like Lucky Fulcrum never fully comply with the Franchise Rule, and most will beat a hasty retreat when it is even mentioned. Some dubious promoters will argue that their business is "exempt" or other such nonsense. Never believe it. With few exceptions, an opportunity will generally be considered a "franchise" whenever goods or services are supplied by the offering person or entity, whenever training or help with sales are part of the deal, and whenever the investor is required to pay $500 or more within the first six months of operation. Most scammers will be exposed by their evasive response (or non-response) to this simple letter:

> Thank you for speaking with me regarding _____. I am interested in learning more about your business and the opportunity you are marketing. Kindly send me, for careful review by my legal and financial advisors, all disclosure documents and proposed contracts as required under the FTC's Franchise Rule (16 CFR Part 436), "Disclosure Requirements and Prohibitions Concerning Franchising and Business Opportunity Ventures," effective date 10/21/1979. Please also send me any other literature and reports you may have about your business along with detailed biographical summaries or vitaes on the company's principals. Thanks again.

Needless to say, had Vernon Yost sent Robby Jones such a letter, he would never have heard back from him again—sure evidence that Vendor Opportunity Unlimited was nothing but a scam operation.

Even if a company complies with the Franchise Rule, there's no guarantee that the opportunity has any investment merit. I have periodically seen offering memorandums of risky investments with serious inaccuracies and omissions. Remember, just because it's in writing doesn't necessarily mean it's true. Prospective franchisors must verify important disclosures and check all material claims. Investors should insist that all earnings claims be in writing, and they should be alert to what may be missing from any disclosure documents received.

There are many promoters who tiptoe around the law, providing some but never all of the disclosures necessary for a truly informed investment decision. Some swindlers, like Lucky Fulcrum, have become adept at ostensibly complying with the law, not truly but passably, thereby avoiding any criminal consequences for their obvious rip-off schemes. The principle *caveat emptor* bolsters the criminal justice system's unwillingness to pursue such cases, which are difficult and expensive to prosecute, thereby shifting the cases to the civil courts by default. As if in the upside-down world of Alice in Wonderland, the civil courts may actually protect people like Fulcrum, who are legally insulated from personal liability by the firewall of an insolvent corporation without discernible assets. Seemingly unfair at times, our legal system may reflect a cultural bias against those who can't keep their hands on their own wallets—victims who unwittingly preserve and animate the principle of *caveat emptor.* Unscrupulous promoters continually take advantage of the careless and defenseless, and the legal system often lets them. Because these hustlers have little to fear from the criminal justice system, careful due diligence is the only effective way to protect yourself against them.

In franchise deals, due diligence begins by requesting and then examining all required disclosures. Investors, however, should never be impressed or reassured by their length and heft. Words can as easily confuse and mislead as enlighten and explain. Even if a franchise opportunity looks good on paper, an investor must always examine the business in operation by personally visiting existing franchises and speaking with owners and managers face to face. Prospective franchise investors should always ask for a complete list of franchisees, along with their addresses and phone numbers. They should then contact some who are *not* suggested by the franchisor. References strongly promoted by franchisors should always be suspect; they could be "singers," impostors paid to give a glowing recommendation to gullible marks like Vernon.

Having seen what happened to Vernon, readers contemplating a franchise business should be wary of all "opportunities" advertised via newspapers, magazines, radio, and television. I personally believe that 99 percent of those with toll-free numbers are scams. Before even considering making an investment, prudent would-be franchisees should study the franchise industry itself. Trade associations such as the International Franchise Association (www.franchise.org) and the American Association of Franchisees and Dealers (www.aafd.org) have resource centers and knowledgeable advisors to help novices through the risks and complexities of opening a franchise business. Other industry trade associations can also be of immense assistance when buying a business. They can be especially helpful in providing insight about past scandals and scams particular to a given industry. Knowing about the thorny areas helps guide informed individuals about where to dig for more information, irrespective of the business under consideration. Had Vernon, for example, contacted the National Automatic Merchandising Association (www.vending.org), he could have learned all about various vending scams and about the reasonable cost of machines, which would have exposed those offered by Vend-Op as inferior and grossly overpriced. Similarly, had Ferris Dunkel contacted the International Packaged Ice Association (www.packagedice.com), he would have been steered to experts qualified to evaluate Ice Kingdom in the context of industry standards and national trends.

How much due diligence is enough? How many concerns should be examined before proceeding with an investment? The rule now is, the more money invested, the more questions need answering beforehand. This wasn't always the case. Years ago, merger and acquisition (M&A) due diligence simply meant examining an audit report. Now it means plumbing the very bowels of a company and questioning the underlying assumptions of its business. Prior to Enron's collapse and the corporate scandals of 2002, a business's financial disclosures were generally accepted at face value. No longer. Prudent investors now look past the numbers and question the reasons and judgments behind a company's financial statements and the transactions they supposedly summarize. In truth, financial statements rarely reflect a company's actual value.

With the prevalence of incomplete or inaccurate financial reporting, business buyers must be alert for even a hint of accounting irregularities and shaded truth, a much more common problem than outright fraud. Information provided by a seller must be verified independently and not be taken at face value. Furthermore, buyers should never rely solely on information provided by the target company.

Prudent buyers should conduct discreet and independent inquiries, soliciting material information from other knowledgeable sources, including suppliers, distributors, customers, industry experts, and sometimes even competitors.

Too often, the analysis preceding the acquisition of, or investment in, a new business focuses too narrowly on financial matters, neglecting many other critical factors that can affect results, such as environmental exposures, supplier contracts, regulatory issues, potential litigation, and a host of others. These nonfinancial factors, as Ferris Dunkel now knows, can influence the viability of an enterprise and must be evaluated during the due diligence phase, before the negotiation of a binding agreement. Identifying defects should be the primary objective. After all, the assets and positive attributes of a business are almost always visible from the outset of such a transaction. The aim is to obtain full disclosure of the relative strengths and weaknesses of a business or investment opportunity. To that end, proper due diligence hinges on asking the right questions and insisting on complete and accurate answers on widely ranging subjects, about everything from fixed assets to environmental concerns.

Every due diligence investigation is different, tailored to the transaction. Obviously, the due diligence required for purchasing a pizza parlor differs considerably from that required for the acquisition of a major manufacturing company. I have seen acquisitions that required an army of professionals working for more than a year to complete the due diligence. Small deals obviously do not require that level of analysis, though the underlying principle remains the same: prudent investment requires a thorough understanding of the deal. To minimize the risk of failure and disappointment, all aspects of an investment must be objectively reviewed beforehand. When a due diligence investigation is complete, there should be no secrets.

An impartial, unbiased approach to due diligence is essential. Focusing only on the positive aspects of a deal can be as risky as focusing only on the defects. The lead investigator, preferably a friendly person with strong interpersonal skills, should be constrained to gather relevant information without expressing opinions or conclusions, avoiding arguments with the seller or the seller's team over incomplete, misleading, or even false information. Confrontations should be left to the attorneys and the principal investors. Due diligence preferably should not become contentious. Good will improves the flow of information and forestalls misunderstandings. Serious wrangling should be reserved for final negotiations, after due diligence has been concluded.

Due diligence gives a buyer more control over the acquisition process, and should have a favorable impact on price and other contractual matters. The information obtained from due diligence, if it does not discourage further investment interest, enables skillful attorneys to draft contracts with appropriate representations and warranties to protect their clients. Unwanted liabilities can often be contractually avoided or mitigated, sometimes by structuring the transaction as a sale of assets instead of equity. Indemnifications and other concessions can also be negotiated and written into the closing documents. In short, proper due diligence helps attorneys do their jobs well.

Those readers experienced in mergers and acquisitions will surely think this short narrative on due diligence far too simplistic, ignoring as it does the analytical complexities of major transactions. I readily agree. My personal due diligence checklist exceeds 100 pages. Indeed, a comprehensive "how-to" explanation of due diligence would be a book in itself. I have instead tried to demonstrate why everyone must be careful when considering investments. Readers must expect and anticipate serious flaws in every deal and look for them determinedly before investing a dime. If the risks are great and the rewards too small, you should walk away without regrets. There will always be other opportunities.

□ □ □ **CAUTIONARY TIPS:**

- Approach due diligence from the viewpoint that there is a "deal breaker" waiting to be discovered, and then systematically go about uncovering it.
- Never let hopes and emotions influence the due diligence process.

- Seek competent professional advice before becoming contractually obligated.

- Remember that you may be negotiating with someone untrustworthy.

- Negotiations should be cut off if an obvious misrepresentation is discovered. Where there is one lie, there are surely others.

- Successful investment (versus lucky betting) requires thorough investigation, assessment, analysis, and astute judgment of future risk and return.

- Never accept representations without verification.

- Look before you leap.

Remember, oftentimes the greatest cost in a deal gone bad is emotional. Over time, people learn to accept major losses caused by acts of God, such as floods or tornadoes that sweep away homes or businesses. On the other hand, most people never completely recover from big losses they have brought on themselves, especially when they see clearly all the things they might have done to prevent them.

CHAPTER 3

Negligent Hiring

□ □ □ CASE #1 DANNY BILTMORE:
   "OLD PAL, BAD EMPLOYEE"

For Danny Biltmore, the best part of his twenty-fifth college reunion was renewing his friendship with Hank Phipps, whom he hadn't seen since graduation. They had been in the same fraternity and as young men had enjoyed many laughs and even more lagers together. Charming, fun-loving Hank had been among the most popular and admired people in their graduating class. He was one of those rare individuals who exuded warmth and positive energy, triggering smiles and good feelings from everyone he met. Now, twenty-five years later, Danny still recognized Hank's old charisma, though his friend was more subdued than he remembered, and sipped soda water instead of pounding beers as he had in the past.

Danny learned during a quiet conversation that weekend that Hank had had a successful sales career with a variety of corporations, but hadn't worked for the last half-year after going through a painful divorce. Anguish clouded his face as he briefly and hesitantly described the end of his marriage. He confided his deep regret that he hadn't been a more devoted husband. "I was just too selfish and self-absorbed," he divulged, his eyes cast downward. Then Hank perked up and cheerily said he was ready to start anew and find another job, feeling much more "balanced" following what he called his six-month "sabbatical from the workday world."

Before drifting off to sleep that night, Danny thought about his own marriage and the strain his career had placed on his wife and children. He owned a small distribution company and spent considerable time traveling and entertaining customers. For years, his wife had badgered him to hire a salesman to help shoulder the load, but he had always rebuffed her requests, claiming he couldn't afford it. Danny could no longer use this excuse because his company had become very successful. After listening to Hank and with jolting clarity, he realized suddenly that his own marriage was at risk of failing. As his mind raced, going over his conversation with Hank, it occurred to him that his wife no longer pestered him for more of his time, a telling indication that she'd begun to disengage emotionally.

While lying sleepless that night, Danny felt as if the heavens had delivered his old friend back to him for a reason. He recalled the old Zen saying, "When the student is ready to learn, the teacher will appear." Hank's tale of marital woe powerfully inspired Danny to become more attentive to his wife and children, more responsive to their needs. He resolved to make more time for those he truly loved. Danny decided to offer Hank a job as senior sales associate and assign him about a dozen established accounts. Even after sorting all of this out, Danny still couldn't sleep, as his excitement and anticipation of good things to come kept him awake even deeper into the night.

Without preamble or hesitancy, Danny offered Hank a job on the spot when they met up the next morning. They spent the next few hours talking about the business and the chances for expanding sales. Though warm and appreciative, Hank remained reserved during their long discussion, as if uncertain and wary of the opportunity. Danny continued to work on Hank throughout the day as they took part in more of the reunion festivities, and then when they met again for a late supper. In something of a role reversal, it was Danny who exuded bonhomie, enthusing about the proposed alliance and the great fun they'd have working together.

When Hank demurred, asking for time to think about it, Danny heaped further incentives on top of an already generous offer. Inwardly, Danny had concluded that his marriage—indeed his very happiness— depended on Hank coming to work for him. He envisioned Hank attracting new customers and cementing profitable deals with his charm and sociability, while he would spend more evenings at home at long last, the good father and husband.

With single-minded persistence, Danny eventually persuaded Hank to join his firm, and they sealed their agreement with a hearty handshake. Ecstatic, Danny signaled the waitress and ordered champagne to toast their future. Hank initially tried to dissuade him, saying he'd "cut back" on alcohol since his divorce, but Danny would not be deterred. They shared one glass . . . then another . . . then another. Danny marveled as the old Hank, the affable and fun-loving guy he remembered so well, reappeared after consuming a bottle of champagne. Jovial and raucous, the two old friends spent the last day of their college reunion happily celebrating their past and their future.

A month later and only two weeks after starting his new job, Hank ran a red light in the early evening and collided with a Mercedes, killing the driver and seriously injuring the driver's wife. Hank was also badly injured in the accident, breaking both legs and dislocating a hip. Tests at the hospital revealed that his blood alcohol level was almost twice the legal limit at the time of the accident.

Investigation and Aftermath

Sadly, Danny's hiring his old college chum did not free up more time for him to spend with his wife and children as he'd hoped. Just the reverse: the legal and financial problems ensuing from the accident consumed Danny's time, money, and ultimately his peace of mind.

A police investigator interviewed Hank in the hospital two days after the accident. Despondent and in considerable pain despite the powerful medications he was taking, Hank disclosed that just before the accident he'd been entertaining a prospective customer at a nearby restaurant. He also named Danny Biltmore as his employer, identified the restaurant, and confirmed that the dinner and drinks had been paid by company credit card. All this information was attached to the accident report in a lengthy narrative handwritten by the investigator.

The driver who'd been killed was a successful forty-five-year-old investment banker who'd earned $400,000 the year before his death. His injured wife eventually recovered but had to endure multiple operations for moderately disfiguring facial injuries. Within weeks of the tragic accident, the wife engaged an attorney who quickly filed suit against Hank Phipps. Five weeks later, the attorney amended the original complaint, naming both Danny Biltmore's company and the restaurant as additional defendants.

Danny's attorney, anticipating the lawsuit, engaged an experienced investigator to help identify the legal exposures and potential liabilities arising from the facts of the case. Such an investigation, reasoned Danny's attorney, might uncover mitigating (or even exonerating) information that could help shape a defense. Unfortunately, what the investigator discovered and reported back dismayed the attorney and horrified Danny, who knew instantly that he faced potential ruin. The facts shifted their thinking from vigorous defense to damage control. Danny's mistakes would certainly cost him; the only question was how much.

The investigator had begun by interviewing the waitress who'd served Hank and the prospective customer just before the accident. She confirmed that Hank had been drinking heavily the night of the accident. The restaurant produced the company credit card and dinner receipts indicating two patrons had consumed a bottle of wine, two martinis, and an after-dinner cognac. The restaurant had a reputation for generous servings, so the actual ounces of liquor consumed likely exceeded the number of drinks. The investigator then found and interviewed the person Hank had been entertaining, the purchasing agent for a local company Danny had suggested to Hank as a potential customer. The man, who'd read about the accident in the local newspaper, thanked his lucky stars he hadn't also been killed. This prospective customer, who drank only one glass of wine that evening, had been so concerned by Hank's inebriation that he'd refused to drive home with him and called a cab instead.

One comment by the purchasing agent included in the investigative report particularly worried Danny's attorney. The witness disclosed that Hank had encouraged him to eat and drink heartily, telling him that "his boss" (presumably Danny) had provided him with a substantial budget to entertain clients and "make sure they had a good time." Hank had urged him to "drink up," but he'd declined, turned off by Hank's progressively drunken behavior.

The investigator then checked into Hank Phipps's driving record. Hank had three prior DUI convictions in the previous three years. Just the year before, he'd been arrested and convicted for drunken driving, failing to yield, and leaving the scene after another accident.

The circumstances of that case were almost identical to the fatal accident, except no one was killed or hurt that time. Hank's most recent conviction had resulted in a thirty-day jail sentence, the suspension of his driver's license for a year, and court-ordered participation in a three-month, in-hospital alcoholism treatment program. Hank's "sabbatical from the workday world" had in fact been spent mostly in jail and the hospital, drying out. During this time period, Hank's wife divorced him. Divorce court records revealed Hank had been fired from three jobs in as many years for problems related to excessive drinking—a central concern in the court's awarding custody of the children to his ex-wife.

The investigator learned another complicating fact: Hank's driver license had been reinstated just before he went to work for Danny. He'd neglected, however, to obtain the insurance coverage mandated by state law, though he attested he'd done so on the application form. Apparently, Hank had been having trouble securing insurance because of his abysmal driving record.

Negotiated settlements often say more about an attorney's skill than successful outcomes at trial. Danny's attorney knew that it was imperative to settle the lawsuit as quickly as possible, preferably before all the facts became known to the other side. Given the evidence, a jury would almost certainly find Danny's company negligent, and possibly award punitive damages, for failing to check Hank's background and driving record before hiring him. Like all employers, Danny had a legal duty not to hire anyone constituting a known danger to others. Hank's driving record and history of alcoholism indicated that another accident could be seen as reasonably foreseeable.

After two long and upsetting discussions with his attorney, Danny reluctantly agreed to a large structured settlement, half paid by the insurance company (at the policy limit) and the other half paid by Danny's company. The plaintiff's attorney went after Danny's company during the settlement negotiations and all but ignored Hank. Despite Hank's obvious personal liability for the accident, he had few assets and no insurance, and consequently had little role in how the case played out. Parties in lawsuits invariably try to place the greatest blame on those with the deepest pockets. Hank's negligence in driving drunk without insurance was, from the plaintiff's viewpoint, less egregious than the negligence of Danny's company for failing to check him out before sending him on a sales assignment that presumed alcohol consumption. Even so, Danny had a difficult time accepting that he'd have to pay the entire settlement while Hank, who had been largely responsible, paid nothing.

A practical man, Danny's attorney eventually persuaded him to agree to the settlement to ensure the company's survival, rather than risk an adverse outcome in the courtroom and possibly lose everything. Though Danny thought he had ample insurance coverage, he had to accept the painful fact that in the eyes of insurance companies, some lives are worth considerably more than others, based on the present-day, discounted-value of estimated potential future earnings. A million dollar auto insurance policy, though sufficient for most lawsuits, is grossly inadequate for damages arising from the wrongful death of someone with earnings as high as a forty-five-year-old investment banker. Unfortunately for Danny and his company, Hank had killed someone both relatively young and earning a bundle—a mouthwatering combination for plaintiff lawyers working on contingency.

Danny's attorney did a masterful job striking a deal that financially hurt Danny but allowed him to stay in business. Danny was also lucky that the plaintiff just wanted to be done with the lawsuit and get on with her life. In fact, she accepted far less than the case was probably worth. Danny suffered other painful consequences in addition to the financial hit of the settlement. His marriage took a terrible turn for the worse during the lawsuit. Even the best marriages often become rocky and turbulent during high-stakes lawsuits, while troubled marriages usually get torn asunder. Before the lawsuit, Danny's wife tolerated his spousal shortcomings, which were softened by the affluent lifestyle made possible by his business success. When their financial future became shaky and less secure, their relationship unraveled. Ironically, Danny had hired Hank with an eye toward saving his marriage, but in fact it hastened its demise.

Hank Phipps never worked another day for Danny Biltmore. He succeeded in obtaining workers' compensation coverage for his injuries and collected benefits for more than a year. After he recovered sufficiently to appear in court, Hank was convicted on multiple counts stemming from the accident and spent a year in prison. Since his release, Hank reportedly has remained sober. Danny and Hank, now former friends, haven't spoken since shortly after the accident.

□ □ □ **CASE #2: RON#2—RON AND RUTH HOLLIDAY:**
 "ALWAYS HIRE A PRO"

Ron and Ruth Holliday's new nightclub was the hottest place in town, filled each night with mobs of patrons gyrating on the dance floor and clamoring for drinks. After only a month in business, the club was grossing more than $7,000 each night, nearly half of that pure profit. Their formula was simple: loud music, cheap beer. Located in the city's warehouse district, the club occupied what had once been the hayloft for a livery stable built in the nineteenth century. It had wood-plank floors, high ceilings with enormous timber beams, and dramatic lighting hidden in the rafters. A pulsating sound system made the entire building and everything in it reverberate. Appropriately, Ron and Ruth called their club simply, "The Loft."

A surprise inspection by the fire marshal put a damper on their enterprise. Upon finding that the number of patrons in the club exceeding that allowed by code, he issued a citation and directed the club to limit occupancy or face immediate closure. After the official left, Ron and Ruth discussed the problem with their bartender, who suggested hiring a burly doorman to keep count and restrict access when the place filled up. The bartender said he knew the "perfect person" for the job, a semipro boxer who sometimes worked as a bouncer.

The next day, Ron and Ruth interviewed Tim Buckham, nicknamed "Tiny," a towering, tightly wound wedge of muscle with icy eyes set in an expressionless face. He was well groomed and dressed in stylish clothes consistent with those worn by the club's hip young clientele. Though courteous and respectful, Tiny was painfully reserved, almost evasive, throughout the interview, answering questions only perfunctorily. Despite having some misgivings, Ron and Ruth hired Tiny on the spot. Their powers of rationalization overwhelmed their intuition, which warned them that something wasn't right about the man. Awed by his intimidating presence, they rationalized that they needed someone who commanded respect, not someone with strong interpersonal skills. They believed they were hiring a pro, someone with obvious physical training and military discipline. Tiny had re-assuringly mentioned that he'd been a Navy SEAL, one of the few things he'd disclosed about himself at the interview.

His first evening on the job, Tiny stationed himself at the door and tallied those entering with a hand-held counter. Just before nine o'clock, the club reached its occupancy limit and Tiny barricaded the door, letting people in only as others left. An impatient crowd waited out front, growing larger by the minute, and three unruly college boys started giving Tiny a hard time. Like an American version of a British Royal Guard, Tiny ignored them, standing erect with his arms crossed and his eyes focused on the fire hydrant across the street.

The three young men hopped around and barked like dogs, try-ing to get some kind of response from the impassive man blocking the door. Tiny seemed not to notice them. Two women left and Tiny gestured that two of the college jerks could enter. Unwilling to be left behind, the third in line also tried to pass, but Tiny grabbed him by the arm and stopped him. Trying to pull free, the big but pudgy guy yelled he was with the two who'd just gone inside. Without warning, Tiny flung him backwards and, with a gelatinous crunch, the young man landed on his backside.

Excited by the unfolding street theater, the waiting crowd pushed forward to watch. The young man popped up and started cursing Tiny. Without warning, Tiny punched him hard in the mouth, then again, and then stomped him repeatedly after he fell to the ground. Several bystanders, appalled by what was happening, stepped forward and tried to intervene to keep Tiny from killing him. Tiny then went ber-serk: like a cornered animal, he swung wildly at anyone and everyone, even at those scrambling out of his way. Someone in the crowd had the good sense to call 911 on a cellular phone.

A police car arrived within minutes, followed by a roving television news team alerted by their police radio scanner. The cameraman video-taped some dramatic footage of the police subduing and handcuffing Tiny, who continued to struggle while being dragged to the police car.

Several witnesses breathlessly recounted on camera how Tiny had snapped. The news team also videotaped the injured man getting hoisted into an ambulance. Later, some drunken patrons leaving the club behaved shamelessly in front of the still-present camera. The late night news shows on every station in town led off their broadcasts with lurid stories about violence and degeneracy at The Loft.

Investigation and Aftermath

For the next week, the local television stations ran news reports about the melee at The Loft, replaying the same sensational video footage again and again. The newspapers wrote about what had happened, and the town's major daily also published an editorial denouncing the underage drinking and unruly behavior in the warehouse district. In response to the political uproar, the local liquor control board suspended and later revoked The Loft's license for serving alcohol to minors.

Before even leaving the hospital, the seriously injured man engaged a tenacious personal injury attorney, who himself hired an investigator to interview witnesses and check Tiny's background in anticipation of filing a civil lawsuit against Tiny and his employer. Criminal records revealed that Timothy "Tiny" Buckham had two prior arrests for assault and battery and another for disorderly conduct. Just three months earlier, he'd been indicted for beating up his girlfriend, sending her to the hospital with multiple fractures and contusions. Doctors treating her had alerted the authorities. The criminal felony charges against Tiny were eventually dropped in a plea bargain. Tiny avoided jail time by agreeing to pay a fine and undergo anger-control counseling. Just two days before he took the job at The Loft, Tiny's psychologist informed the court Tiny had missed his last five sessions, and a warrant was issued for his arrest. In addition to reviewing court records, the investigator interviewed Tiny's neighbors, friends, and former employers. From multiple witnesses, the investigator learned that Tiny had a long history of bizarre behavior, violence, and delusional thinking. He often boasted he'd served as a Navy SEAL and boxed as a professional. Neither was true.

The injured young man's attorney quickly filed a negligent hiring/negligent supervision lawsuit against The Loft, claiming the defendant "knew or should have known" that Tiny posed a substantial risk of harm to others. The plaintiff sought $2 million in actual and punitive damages for his client's numerous injuries, including serious neurological and cognitive deficits. The lawsuit received much media attention when filed, and the local television stations used it as an opportunity to replay the videotapes from the night of the incident. At trial, the jury found for the plaintiff and awarded him more than $1 million dollars in punitive and compensatory damages. Because of the lawsuit and liquor license problems, The Loft never reopened and, in the end, Ron and Ruth Holliday lost everything they had, filing for personal bankruptcy soon after the trial.

Buckham served sixteen months in state prison after pleading guilty to a reduced charge in another plea bargain. After his release, he reportedly left the state and eventually got a job as a security guard at an apartment complex for the elderly somewhere in the Sunbelt. Hopefully, the 'early-bird-special' crowd will be less likely to light his very short fuse.

□ □ □ **CASE #3—GREG AUSTIN:**
　　 "NO EXPERIENCE NECESSARY"

Greg Austin thought Judd Horner would be perfect for the new job he was creating at his company. Though Greg didn't know Judd well, he liked and enjoyed being around him. They regularly saw each other at the local fitness club where, as avid racquetball players, both played in the amateur league. Judd was an unusually gifted athlete, intensely competitive but always fun and good-natured on the court. He brought out the best in his opponents.

After one unusually spirited match, won by Judd, the two men shot the breeze while cooling down. During their conversation, Greg learned that Judd was looking for a part-time position because his employer, a local construction company, had cut his hours for lack of work. Coincidentally, Greg had been looking for someone to help launch a new business idea. Greg owned and operated a firm that waterproofed and repaired moisture-damaged basements. It had recently occurred to him that radon detection and mediation could be an excellent complementary business. Radon mediation was not unlike basement waterproofing: both involved sealing off spaces from something unwanted and harmful.

On impulse, Greg offered Judd a part-time job installing radon detectors in people's basements. "Installing" was perhaps an overstatement considering what was actually involved. The job simply required opening and placing a radon detector in the center of a basement and retrieving it about a week later for analysis at an accredited laboratory. In fact, any responsible ten-year-old could qualify as a "radon detection technician." Greg figured Judd might make a good salesman with his friendly personality. Besides, if Judd didn't work out, he could always let him go. Essentially, Greg saw Judd's hiring as a no-risk deal.

About two weeks after Greg hired Judd, a policeman investigating a "criminal matter" stopped by to ask a few questions. The police detective requested the name of the employee who'd placed a radon detector at Ms. Eileen Maple's home two days earlier. Greg told him it was Judd Horner, but got nothing in return when he asked why he wanted to know this information, which triggered his sense of unease. The detective also requested a physical description of Judd, as well as his home address, Social Security number, and other identifying information. He then asked if Judd ever wore unusual turquoise athletic shoes with black striping. Greg confirmed that he did, adding offhandedly that only an athletic showboat like Judd could wear such flamboyant shoes and not get teased. The detective did not smile, as if silently admonishing Greg that this was no laughing matter.

The policeman concluded the interview by asking if he knew Judd's whereabouts at that moment, which Greg did not. He responded that Judd only worked part-time, and he hadn't seen him since the day in question. Before leaving, the detective directed Greg not to contact Judd or tip him off that the police had been asking about him, adding that Greg could face obstruction of justice charges if he even thought about doing so. For the rest of the afternoon, Greg had a growing sense of foreboding, as if something grotesque and sinister lay just ahead. The next day, he was shocked to learn that Judd Horner had been arrested and jailed on multiple charges, including assault and battery, larceny, and breaking and entering, among others. At first, Greg was slow to comprehend how seriously he'd be affected by Judd's criminal misconduct.

Investigation and Aftermath

Judd's turquoise shoes linked him to the crime. Eileen Maple, the widow who'd been victimized, could not identify her assailant, but remembered the turquoise shoes as those worn by the man who'd placed the radon detector in her basement earlier that day. Armed with a warrant, the police arrested Judd, searched his apartment, and found everything taken from Ms. Maple's home. They also found the turquoise shoes and took them as evidence. Eileen Maple had accurately described those shoes in a lengthy statement to the police that detailed what had happened to her.

According to Ms. Maple, Judd Horner had made her feel uncomfortable from the moment he entered her house to test for radon. He had walked around examining her artwork and heirloom silver, touching pieces without permission as if an invited guest, unctuously praising all the nice things she owned. Staring too intently and standing too close, Judd seemed overly curious about her, even impudently asking if she lived alone. He had been in no hurry whatsoever to complete his assignment and continue on his way. Gracious though she was, Eileen Maple finally had to cut him off and asked him to leave, saying she had an appointment in an hour and just enough time to get ready. Actually, she had no plans to go anywhere and just said that to get him out of her house. Apparently, Judd took her at her word; he later confessed that he'd returned two hours later, thinking she'd left, and forced open the back door.

Wearing a ski mask and a baggy sweatshirt, Judd first ransacked the ground floor, stuffing sterling silver, carved ivory, and other valuables in a nylon bag. Eileen Maple, who'd been resting upstairs, heard noises and got up to investigate. When she opened her bedroom door she found a masked intruder standing before her, seemingly as surprised as she. For a brief moment the two gaped at each other, before the man grabbed her and forced her to the ground. Using duct tape, he quickly trussed her like a Thanksgiving turkey, securing her arms behind her back and her ankles to her wrists, then silenced her by winding tape around her head and across her mouth. Breathing heavily, the masked man dropped her head to the floor. Convinced he'd kill her next, Eileen Maple whimpered, trembled, and (to her shame) lost control of her bladder. Waiting for the blow that never came, she stared at his feet . . . at his turquoise shoes.

Eileen Maple never contemplated a civil suit against Greg Austin's company until the sentencing hearing at which she learned that Judd Horner had a prior criminal history. The judge alluded to his prior convictions when she sentenced him to an eight-year prison sentence on a single felony count. All the other criminal charges against him were dropped in a plea bargain. Looking cocky and smug, Judd had winked at her while being led away in handcuffs from the courtroom.

The week after Judd's sentencing, Eileen obsessed about the fact that Judd had a prior criminal history. How could a reputable company have sent that fiend into her home? How could they have been so irresponsible? Suspecting she'd never regain her peace of mind without getting some answers, she met with her attorney, an old family friend with a distinguished law firm. He engaged an investigator to check out Judd Horner's background. The investigator quickly and easily learned that Judd had a long history of criminal mischief dating back to his childhood. Even his own parents had washed their hands of him. Judd had been in and out of juvenile detention homes and (later) jail for a smorgasbord of offenses, including car theft, drug possession, sexual imposition, and burglary. His most recent employer, a residential construction contractor, had fired him after catching him loading company tools into his car. In his defense, Judd had said he was only "borrowing" the tools and had planned to return them. The contractor did not believe him. Two other prior employers also denounced Judd in conversations with the investigator, both saying he was a liar and utterly untrustworthy. Both suspected, but couldn't prove, that Judd had stolen items of value from them.

Working on contingency, Eileen Maple's attorney filed a negligent hiring lawsuit against Greg Austin's company. During discovery, he learned, of course, that Greg had failed to conduct any kind of background investigation before hiring Judd. Having the upper hand, he bludgeoned Greg mercilessly in deposition, and Greg's attorney almost begged to settle the case the following day. Eileen's attorney did a brilliant job of squeezing Greg while protecting Eileen from the usual stresses of civil litigation. In fact, he later acknowledged that he would have dropped the lawsuit to keep her from being deposed, let alone subject her to testifying at trial. She was simply too broken and vulnerable by the experience to be exposed to a trial attorney's onslaught. The amount of the final settlement was kept confidential, though rumored to be well into the six figures. Whatever the actual amount, the settlement certainly set Greg back financially. He dropped his fitness club membership soon after the case settled, presumably to reduce personal expenses.

□ □ □ **COMMENTARY AND ANALYSIS**

When employers hire people, they also hire their problems. As these three cases illustrate, hiring people with serious, identifiable problems can be the costliest of business blunders, particularly when problems are easily identifiable and should entirely disqualify someone from being hired. Employers must always remember that they have a duty to exercise reasonable care when hiring someone who, because of the nature of the position they fill, may pose a threat of injury to others. Legal liability arising from this duty hinges on whether the risk of an employee harming another person was reasonably foreseeable. Given Hank's drinking and driving problems, it was indeed foreseeable that he'd have another accident if hired for a job that involved consuming alcohol and driving. Given Tiny's violent history and psychological problems, it was reasonably foreseeable he'd hurt someone if hired as a doorman/bouncer. Given Judd's criminal history, it was reasonably foreseeable he'd steal and possibly worse if he had unsupervised access to people's homes.

Over the years, I have seen scores of businesses lose large sums by hiring unqualified people with seriously troubled pasts. Not one of these business disasters had to happen. If those companies had only conducted background investigations beforehand, they would have discovered disqualifying problems in the applicants' pasts and presumably would not have hired them. Employers should think of pre-employment investigations not as an option, but as an obligation. When making hiring decisions, employers must always remember that the best predictor of future behavior is past behavior. In fact, the courts follow this dictum in determining if the injuries or damages at issue in negligent hiring suits were "reasonably foreseeable."

Many businesspeople (and undoubtedly some readers) have difficulty fathoming that they can be held liable for the acts of employees outside the scope of their employment. Nearly everyone can understand how Ruth and Ron had to face the legal consequences for Tiny's violent outburst. After all, they had hired him specifically to stand guard, though they'd never expected him to pummel someone mercilessly as part of his job assignment. The court found Ron and Ruth liable under the doctrine of *respondeat superior,* wherein employers are responsible for wrongful acts by employees in the course and scope of their employment. Danny's liability for Hank's accidentally killing the banker and Greg's liability for Judd's criminal acts against Eileen arose differently, because their employees' wrongful acts, over which they had little or no control, occurred outside the scope of their employment. Danny and Greg were legally liable, however, because by hiring Hank and Greg they placed others (i.e. the banker and Eileen) in harm's way. In legal terms, their negligence was the proximate cause of the banker's death and Eileen's victimization.

In order to prevail in negligent hiring court cases, plaintiffs must first prove that the employer's negligence was the proximate cause of their injuries or property losses. To build a case of negligence, the plaintiff must examine what the employer knew or reasonably could have known about the employee's background, work history, and criminal record before the employee harmed the plaintiff. Under the law, ignorance is never a defense; in fact, ignorance nearly always supports a finding of negligence. Easily discoverable prior criminal and behavioral problems serve as persuasive evidence that the harm caused by an employee was predictable. For the employer, protection from negligent hiring lawsuits arises by making reasonable inquiries into the background of prospective employees before hiring them. To be safe, employers should investigate every prospective employee, though the scope of the investigation depends on the position to be filled.

The nature of the job dictates how carefully an applicant's background should be examined before being hired. For example, an employer could hire almost anyone, whatever his background, to dig postholes alone on a vacant ranch in the middle of nowhere. No harm to anyone could possibly be "foreseeable" by hiring a miscreant for such a position. (I say that with the following caveat: never underestimate a lawyer's ability to argue a "cause of action.") Certain employers, however, are legally held to a higher duty of care by the nature of their business or the position being filled, and must evaluate applicants and investigate their backgrounds more thoroughly. Utmost care must be exercised when filling jobs involving frequent, unsupervised contact with people, particularly when they are society's most vulnerable, such as children, the sick, and the elderly. Many states now require teachers, nursing home aides, camp counselors, and child-care providers to undergo comprehensive criminal background checks.

To protect others as well as themselves, employers should always check an applicant's criminal history for any job requiring an employee to enter homes or meet people alone and unsupervised. From their social interaction at the fitness club, Greg Austin thought he knew Judd Horner, but in fact he did not know him at all; Greg simply had a superficial impression of Judd that turned out to be entirely wrong and misguided. Impressions should never be mistaken for knowledge, particularly when filling jobs that require a higher standard of care. Greg should have followed selection procedures consistently applied to all job applicants, regardless of whether he "knew" any of them beforehand. Such procedures, depending on the position, can include job analyses, detailed application forms, skill and integrity testing, interviews, reference and background checks, medical examinations, drug testing, and criminal checks. Greg Austin, if nothing more, should have checked Judd's criminal and driving record, since the job of "radon tester" involved entering homes unsupervised and driving on company time to get there. Had he done so, Greg certainly would have quickly learned that Judd was a seasoned criminal, a man to be avoided at all costs.

Pressured by business needs to make quick decisions, employers often fill positions in haste or on impulse, relying more on wishful thinking than genuine insight. Danny's fond memories of Hank from twenty-five years ago were of little value in determining his professional competence or identifying his shortcomings. Ron and Ruth abandoned all discernment by trusting the "recommendation" of their bartender, who actually knew little about Tiny and nothing about his troubled past. Meanwhile, Greg mistook Judd's sociable disposition on the racquetball court as evidence of character and integrity. In truth, each of these employers relied on false or inadequate information to predict the future performance of those they hired. But as history proves time and again, predictions are more likely to come true when based on good information, not on hopes and wishes, and the only way to develop good information about job applicants is to examine their past. After all, people will generally not perform better, work harder, or behave differently than they have previously.

Most employers spend too much time qualifying a candidate, making a case that someone is right for the job by focusing more on their virtues than faults. Though misguided, this approach is understandable, since well-adjusted, capable, and productive employees nearly all have backgrounds free from serious problems and controversies. Paradoxically, identifying the best applicants in fact requires probing more for disqualifying than qualifying information. Before extending trust, an employer must first identify those who are undeserving of it.

As a professional, I always begin a background investigation assuming there is something disqualifying in the subject's past, and then I doggedly look for it. I search for dark clouds, not silver linings. All employers should adopt this approach if they want to protect themselves from the gravest hiring mistakes. Since a troubled past foretells a troubled future, a healthy suspicion of all applicants is a prudent safeguard. Personal success, after all, depends on steering clear of seriously troubled people like Hank, Tiny, and Judd, keeping them out of your life and your business, and never giving them the slightest chance to cause you harm or grief. Savvy businesspeople hire only the deserving and let their competitors hire the troublemakers, who can then deal with the losses and lawsuits that often follow.

How should employers look for disqualifying information about applicants, particularly for those jobs requiring a higher standard of care in protecting the public? How does one check criminal and driving records? What are the steps employers should take to meet the legal standard that a background check must be "reasonable" to hold up as an affirmative defense against a negligence hiring suit? Unfortunately, the answers to these questions vary from case to case, influenced by the applicant, the job, and the jurisdiction. Consulting your attorney is the best place to start, particularly to find the specifics in your particular area. Certain principles and guidelines, however, apply for most cases.

Typical pre-employment background checks are usually straight-forward, but some can be confoundingly complex, requiring as much art as science to find out the truth about a person. A good background investigator should have a subtle and inquisitive mind with the ability to look beyond the obvious, follow leads, and listen to what is said and isn't said when talking to people. For pre-employment checks, their job is to verify an applicant's disclosures and also to uncover concealed information that might be disqualifying. (This is why the most effective investigators—rather than being the shady, secretive types that populate movies and TV—are usually friendly people with superb communication skills, who have a knack for interviewing people tactfully yet openly.) Whether employers conduct these investigations themselves or hire an outside firm to do it for them, the underlying principles and steps are essentially the same.

First, employers should always disclose to applicants that they will be subjected to a background investigation before being hired. This disclosure alone will be sufficient to screen out most bad apples who won't bother completing the application process, believing their unsavory past will inevitably be discovered. If the employers in the preceding cases had done this, Judd and Tiny would likely have withdrawn themselves from consideration. Also, Hank might have been more forthcoming about his alcohol problems and prior jail sentence.

Many (if not most) employers feel uncomfortable telling prospective employees that they will be investigated, thinking that such transparent suspicion and distrust will be off-putting. They worry they might offend desirable candidates and cause them to reconsider their application entirely—a serious issue when you're concerned about getting the best possible employees. Obviously, employers should not disclose their screening process by saying, "We're going to investigate you inside and out to make sure you're not a crook." Instead, they should say something more like this: "Our business prides itself on the very high standard of integrity and capability of our workforce. We try to hire only the most qualified and upright candidates, those who enjoy working with people of similar caliber. Based on what I know about you so far, I have reason to believe you would fit in nicely in our organization. However, all candidates must pass a thorough background investigation, including reference and criminal history checks, before we make a final hiring decision. We are considering other impressive candidates, but you're certainly in the running, which is why I ask you to authorize further inquiries into your quali-fications and background."

The best candidates will not be offended by such a disclosure. They will welcome having their unblemished history examined, proud that their sterling qualities will become even more apparent. Yet when someone with a troubled past hears this same disclosure, they will become uncomfortable, and some may get defensive, even accusatory, possibly saying, "I have no intention of being subjected to a background investigation, and I have no desire to work for distrustful people who think I might be a criminal." When hearing such responses, employers should never doubt themselves; instead, they should doubt the suit-ability of the applicant. Defiant and defensive comments more often come from people with something to hide—and even if they don't, do you want to hire people who openly question a reasonable request be-fore being hired? How cooperative and agreeable would those people be after they're on the payroll?

As part of the hiring process, employers should require all job appli-cants sign a "release and authorization" form that clearly discloses the nature and scope of the background investigation. This form entitles the employer to probe a candidate's history and provides protection from a variety of legal exposures, such as "invasion of privacy" complaints by unsuccessful and disgruntled candidates. In addition, some states and courts require a signed release of this kind before any criminal records can be furnished to an employer. The release form also ensures partial compliance with the Fair Credit Reporting Act (FCRA), which governs the release of certain personal information, including credit histories. With its authorization and disclosure requirements, the FCRA plays an important role in almost all investigations, a subject examined more fully later in this chapter. In addition to this essential legal form, another similarly worded "release and authorization" should always be imbedded in the application form, usually placed just before the applicant's signature.

The Application Form

All pre-employment background investigations should begin with a completed and signed application form. (Though it may contain useful information, a résumé should never be accepted as a substitute for an application form.) A good application form should require applicants to disclose their complete employment history, credentials, skills, personal identifiers (name and aliases, date of birth, and Social Security number), driver's license number, home addresses for the previous ten years, and military and criminal histories. Applicants should also be required to account for any gaps in employment and disclose their specific reasons for leaving every previous position. The form should always include a statement confirming that the applicant warrants that the information in the application is true and accurate, and by signing, acknowledges that the employer has the right to either reject or dismiss the applicant for "inaccuracies, omissions, misinformation, or dishonesty of any kind." Employers should be careful never to accept an incomplete or unsigned application form.

Of course, employers *must* verify the information provided by applicants on these forms. Applicants routinely lie on applications; studies cited in *HR* magazine indicate that as many as half of all applications contain one or more serious fabrications or exaggerations. A pre-employment background investigation should start by verify-

NEGLIGENT HIRING □ 61

ing the applicant's name and Social Security number. Most honest, law-abiding citizens would be shocked to learn just how many people falsify these in the effort to evade the sheriff, the IRS, unpaid creditors, swindled partners, and former spouses owed money for alimony and child support. Employers should never rely solely on documentation provided by an applicant. Social Security cards and other documentation can easily be forged with scanners and color copiers. Independent verification of an individual's name, Social Security number, date of birth, and current and former addresses can be obtained quickly by ordering a "credit header" or a full consumer credit report, preferably a "merged report" combining the information compiled by all three major credit reporting agencies—TransUnion, Experian (formerly TRW), and Equifax.

The information received from the credit report should be carefully compared with the information provided by the subject on the application form. Always ask yourself, does the information make sense? For example, if a fifty-year-old, American-born job applicant has a Social Security number issued just eight years earlier, this definitely sends up a red flag. What Social Security number did this person use from ages eighteen to forty-two? Only in very rare cases, under strictly circumscribed conditions, will the Social Security Administration issue someone a new Social Security number—for instance, when a stolen Social Security number has been used fraudulently on repeated occasions, causing the legitimate holder serious and continuing financial harm. Even then, the new Social Security number will always be cross-referenced with the old number, which will appear in the subject's credit report. Except in circumstances like these, a questionable date of issue always constitutes a serious red flag.

A consumer credit report will generally list every address associated with the subject, going back ten years or more, and generally includes the dates of residence at each reported address. The addresses supplied by the applicant should be carefully checked against the addresses supplied by the reporting agency. Do the addresses from the subject's application correspond with those in the consumer credit report? Do the dates and locations match? Keep in mind that criminals and deadbeats often try to withhold any information that might conceivably connect them with their unfavorable past.

Over the years, I have seen many instances where a problematic past remains undisclosed in written applications and résumés, replaced by a fabricated, trouble-free history. Usually these fabrications can be exposed. If a credit report reveals a yearlong residency in another state not noted in the application, perhaps there is a simple explanation. The applicant might have regularly visited his aging parents and had bank statements forwarded to their address, thereby linking his Social Security number to their address. On the other hand, the applicant may have conveniently "forgotten" to mention a year spent jailed for criminal activity. Applicants should always be asked about any discrepancies between their credit report and their job application, followed by independent verification of the explanation, no matter how plausible it may seem.

Employers should pay particular attention to gaps in an applicant's employment history, especially those concealed and later revealed, because they may pinpoint periods of disqualifying or even criminal conduct. Employers should be particularly alert to a "taffy pull," wherein an applicant extends the "end date" of one job to link up with the pre-dated start of another, thereby concealing an obvious employment gap. Disclosed gaps should also be examined closely. For example, Danny should have been instantly alert about Hank's supposed six-month "sabbatical." Long employment gaps explained away as extended vacations, spiritual retreats, world travel, novel composition, or family medical problems often cunningly conceal problems or even wrongdoing.

When investigating an applicant's past, uncovering prior criminal behavior should be the highest priority, since (as in the case of Greg Austin) it potentially exposes the employer to disastrous liability. Searching criminal records, however, is often the most complex and inconclusive component of background investigations, even though it's indispensable for identifying and screening out those most likely to cause serious problems. A word of caution: any vendor or private investigator claiming to use a "national criminal database" should be shunned as untrustworthy, because no such a database is available to the public. Only the FBI and local law enforcement have access to a national criminal database, maintained by the National Crime Information Center (NCIC), which by law remains inaccessible to individuals and businesses. In fact, law enforcement officials can use the NCIC database only during official investigations; unauthorized use of the NCIC database will, almost without fail, bring a felony charge against the user.

A comprehensive criminal background check entails searching records on the local and state level, often an imposing task considering there are more than 3,000 county courthouses in America. In addition, every small municipality and county sheriff's department nationwide compiles criminal records. Only a limited number of these repositories have searchable indexes available online. Faced with the sheer number of record-keepers, there is often the chance and occasionally the likelihood of missing something during a criminal search. A seemingly upstanding citizen in one suburban community may have a lengthy arrest and conviction record in an adjoining jurisdiction. Checking the records of the former and not the latter would result in an inaccurate and incomplete profile on that individual. In addition, felony and misdemeanor charges are often dismissed or plea-bargained away. Skilled lawyers often persuade prosecutors to drop a case by portraying their client as emotionally troubled and needing psychological counseling rather than incarceration. And many criminal records are sealed or even expunged, particularly those concerning youths.

Because of these inherent complications, one can rarely be certain that the results of a criminal search are complete and wholly accurate. Even submitting fingerprint cards to various state criminal records repositories for analysis—which is often the best search available—will not guarantee a complete picture of an individual's criminal past. State laws largely govern the availability of official records. Contacting a bureau of criminal investigation in one state will not necessarily identify criminal activity from another that has more restrictive records-access statutes.

Faced with these multiple (and often exasperating) challenges, background investigators are best off identifying those jurisdictions where the subject would have been most likely to commit any unlawful activity and focus their efforts there. Most criminals commit their offenses close to home. Consequently, the best place to look for evidence of criminal activity is in the records of the counties and municipalities where the subject currently resides or has previously resided. This is the primary reason for requesting and then confirming an applicant's current and prior addresses; they direct the investigator to those courthouses and law enforcement departments most likely to contain relevant records. Had Danny simply checked the courthouse records in the county where Hank resided, he'd quickly have found evidence of Danny's drinking and driving offenses. Similarly, Judd's and Tiny's criminal histories could easily have been uncovered had someone just visited the nearest courthouse. Is this a lot of work when filling a position at your company? Perhaps—but consider the nature of the position you are filling, and the potential risk and liability exposure you might be facing should there be problems in an employee's background, and ask yourself if it isn't worth the hassle to ensure you're getting the kind of person you really need.

Whenever checking criminal court records, employers should also consider reviewing civil court records, particularly when filling upper-management positions. Civil litigation searches can be useful in screening out acrimonious malcontents and vexatious litigators. I remember one client who decided against hiring an otherwise impressive candidate for an executive position after learning he'd sued his neighbors for wind-blown leaf debris and charcoal-grill fumes. The company concluded that if the applicant perceived petty annoyances as wrongs worthy of litigation, serious disputes would inevitably arise from normal workplace pressures. In another case, a consulting firm understandably rejected a job applicant after learning his former employer had successfully sued him for "misappropriating" company assets. I still don't understand why the authorities failed to file criminal charges against the perpetrator in that case. Evidence of flagrant and disqualifying misconduct, in other words, may appear in the civil record and not in the criminal record.

A civil litigation search can be particularly helpful in avoiding those most irksome of employees: people with a propensity to litigate. Those who offend easily, those incapable of resolving differences through dialogue, those who blame others for their own shortcomings, and those with a victim mentality are often quick to run to the courthouse to file complaints for perceived wrongs. With each passing year, more angry employees press grievances against employers in court. Of course, employers should never eliminate applicants from consideration for prior litigiousness, or risk being sued themselves. Applicants should simply be told when not selected, "Thanks, but we decided to go with someone else," nothing more.

Of course, a "reasonable" background investigation must do more than simply check court records. State and federal judges have consistently ruled that employers have an obligation to check the driving records of employees before allowing them to drive either a company vehicle or their own vehicle on company business. Application forms should ask job candidates if they have a valid driver's license and, if so, require them to provide the number and state of issue. A large percentage of all employees will use an automobile sometime during the course of their employment, even if only to deliver a package on the way home, thereby exposing their employers to significant liability should an accident occur.

Besides gauging potential liability, checking an applicant's license and driving record is an inexpensive way for employers to verify identity while also providing information concerning an applicant's character. Any employer would surely like to know that an applicant's license had been revoked following four drunken-driving violations in the prior year. Prudent employers should always think twice before hiring hard-core alcoholics, regardless of the position. Danny Biltmore would certainly concur with this advice.

It should go without saying that you should always check an applicant's credentials—including degrees, licenses, and specialized training—before extending a job offer. From my professional experience, I can attest that the more responsible the position, the more likely an applicant will exaggerate or fabricate credentials. I personally have seen scores of cases where an applicant didn't even attend, let alone receive a degree from, the alma mater identified in the application. Verifying an applicant's educational credentials is arguably the best place to begin a background investigation. For one, it is easily done. More importantly, if a check reveals that an applicant has lied about attendance and/or degrees, the investigation can stop right there. Blatant dishonesty regarding educational credentials should immediately disqualify an applicant from further consideration, no matter what the position. If an applicant has lied in this area, an employer can almost be sure the applicant has other reasons to be disqualified as well.

Prior employers should always be contacted to ensure that a background investigation fulfills the standard that it be "reasonable." Prior employers may refuse to cooperate, but a prospective employer has to at least try to get relevant information about an applicant, particularly for jobs requiring a higher standard of care. Efforts to obtain references, even if unsuccessful, should always be well documented. If prior employers are more forthcoming, the background investigator should document their disclosures by taking detailed notes, including the name of the contact and the date of the conversation. For a job requiring unsupervised entry into someone's home, the background investigator must inquire into the applicant's suitability for such a position, asking the references if they know whether the applicant has ever used drugs, abused alcohol, displayed any violent, harassing, or criminal behavior, evidenced any psychological or emotional problems, or exhibited other deficiencies that would call into question the applicant's ability to do the job without causing harm to others. All the employers in the example cases, I assure you, wish they'd contacted prior employers. The problems afflicting Hank, Tiny, and Judd would likely have become evident with only a few telephone calls.

Employers should also take care to look into an applicant's military record, perhaps even more so than an applicant's civilian employment history. It's not uncommon for seriously troubled applicants— criminals and psychopaths alike—to invent impressive military careers. To put this in perspective, the SEAL Identification Team, a group of SEAL veterans who expose impostures, have estimated that the number of people claiming to have been Navy SEALs exceeds the number who actually served by at least a factor of one hundred to one. Furthermore, concocting a military record is a common way of hiding a prison record. In a way, the deception seems perversely understandable considering how both the military and the criminal justice system emphasize discipline! Many delusional nutcases with low self-esteem represent themselves as having a heroic warrior past. Employers should be suspicious when an applicant brags about being "shot up in Nam" or refers obliquely to some "classified" military background. When Tiny told Ron and Ruth he'd been a Navy SEAL, instead of being impressed, they should have been suspicious, and excessively cautious before hiring him as doorman/bouncer—a job requiring a higher standard of care.

Employers should require every applicant who represents having military experience to complete a Military Records Request Form 180. After receiving this completed form by fax, the National Personnel Records Center in St. Louis, Missouri, will generally verify an applicant's military service, rank, and type of discharge over the telephone. The request form should then be mailed to the appropriate military records custodian in order to obtain a more detailed report. If Ron and Ruth had done this before hiring Tiny, they'd have been reminded that Rambo is just a fictional character.

Again, when investigating job applicants, employers must take care to comply with the FCRA or face potentially serious legal consequences. The FCRA stipulates that any employer desiring to utilize a consumer or investigative consumer report must make the subject—whether a job applicant or a current employee—aware that a report may be obtained. The subject must also agree to this in writing beforehand. A "consumer report," as defined by the FCRA, is a report prepared by a consumer reporting agency (CRA) that contains information regarding a subject's credit-worthiness, background, general reputation, lifestyle, and/or personal characteristics. A "consumer report" is generally compiled from records. An "investigative consumer report" contains information compiled from records and interviews of personal references, prior employers, neighbors, and others. Under the FCRA, private investigators, reference-checking companies, and traditional providers of credit information—such as Experian, TransUnion, and Equifax—are all considered CRAs.

Besides requiring written authorization and various disclosures before obtaining a consumer report, the FCRA further mandates that the employer promptly notify the subject if information in a report may result in an adverse employment decision. For example, if a consumer report reveals a poor driving record that may affect a subject's being considered for a truck driver position, the FCRA requires the employer to notify the applicant.

The FCRA places other burdens on employers. After taking an "adverse action" based on a consumer or investigative consumer report, an employer must give the subject notice that action has been taken. Under the law, the "adverse action notice" must include:

1. the name, address, and telephone phone number of the CRA.

2. a statement that the CRA that prepared the report did not make the decision to take the adverse action and cannot give specific reasons for it.

3. notice of the subject's right to dispute the accuracy or completeness of any information furnished by the CRA, and the subject's right to a free copy of the consumer report from the CRA, which must be provided within sixty days upon written request.

Employers must be especially diligent to follow the FCRA regulations to the letter. Using employees to conduct pre-employment investigations and prepare reports on job applicants relieves employers from some, but not all, of the FCRA requirements. Above all, employers should never risk ordering a consumer report without first obtaining written authorization from the subject. If an employer fails to obtain a signed release and authorization form, or fails to disclose adverse actions based on information in a consumer report, the FCRA allows victims to sue for damages in federal court.

Should employers conduct their own pre-employment investigations or should they hire a professional investigative or screening firm to do it for them? Like most things in business, there are pros and cons to each approach. But regardless of the route taken, it behooves all employers to understand the issues and carefully monitor the work.

Everyone in the investigative business occasionally relies on others to search records in other jurisdictions. There is always, however, a leap of faith that those sent to the courthouse will actually examine the records. I sometimes wonder when a searcher reports "no records found," was there truly nothing in the courthouse files or were "no records found" because the searcher spent the day at the diner smoking cigarettes and drinking coffee?

For their own security and peace of mind, employers should seriously consider using only established, experienced firms to outsource investigative work. Though bigger doesn't necessarily mean better, there are advantages in using a larger firm with substantial insurance and deep pockets. If they screw up an investigation, possibly by missing something egregious or by mistakenly linking someone innocent to a criminal conviction, they will face the consequences and presumably will have the financial resources to make it right. Furthermore, hiring a firm with a good reputation adds another layer of protection from negligent hiring lawsuits, arguably meeting the "reasonable care" standard expected by the courts. What more can an employer do, after all, than hire a respectable and experienced investigative firm?

For even more protection, businesses should ask to be named as an "additional insured" on the liability insurance policy of the firm conducting the pre-employment investigations. In today's litigious business world, there is much to be said for shifting risks and liabilities to others.

Obviously, the legal and procedural issues in conducting pre-employment background investigations are complex, with many opportunities for the negligent and uninformed to make serious, even catastrophic mistakes. In very broad terms, I hope I've inspired employers to become more knowledgeable and cautious when hiring people. Entire books and reference volumes have been published detailing the techniques and resources available for conducting background investigations. Instead of providing a "how-to" checklist, I have tried to motivate readers to become more inquiring, more inquisitive about people before accepting them. The truth, keep in mind, is revealed more from what is asked than from what is already known.

□ □ □ **CAUTIONARY TIPS:**

- Qualifying an applicant requires a careful examination of the applicant's past.
- Under the law, it is often not what you know but what you should have known that matters.
- Remember that when you hire people, you also hire their problems.

CHAPTER 4

Workers' Compensation Fraud and Other Investigative Challenges

☐ ☐ ☐ **CASE #1—FRANK RICKMANN:**
   "IT ONLY HURTS WHEN I LAUGH"

Feisty Frank Rickmann was a living example that it's not the size of the man in the fight, but the size of the fight in the man that matters most. Too small for football, he'd dominated his weight class as a high school wrestler two decades ago, qualifying for the state tournament four years in a row.

After graduation, Frank decided to forego college and went to work for his uncle's company, OK Heating & Cooling, a firm specializing in HVAC systems for new home construction. His small size was an advantage because installing furnaces and air conditioners often required him to work in tight spaces. Frank would grapple with fittings and wrenches with the same tenacity he displayed on the wrestling mat. He worked fast without making mistakes and thoroughly enjoyed the work.

Frank eventually purchased OK Heating & Cooling from his uncle and quickly expanded the business, undertaking larger commercial projects and hiring more people. As a hands-on owner, he went from one job site to another supervising the work, often strapping on his tool belt and helping out on the more complicated jobs. Perpetually intense and energetic, he set high standards and demanded the best from everyone. A special *esprit de corps* developed among his employees, who considered themselves "more than OK"; they were the best in the region at their business. Frank changed the company's name from OK to Excelsior Heating & Cooling, which he thought better conveyed his commitment to excellence.

Unfortunately Frank did not excel at sales. Temperamentally, he was incapable of schmoozing potential clients to close deals. Cocky and impatient by nature, he found it irritating, offensive even, having to convince others of his capabilities. Frank had enough self-awareness, however, to know that his prickly personality was costing him money. He wisely decided to hire a full-time salesperson.

In response to a classified advertisement, Jack Stoker appeared at Excelsior's offices as if a gift from heaven. Jack was everything Frank was not: a big man with an easygoing manner and hearty laugh. Jack said he'd been studying for his HVAC certification for the last year while also working as a maintenance engineer at a nearby metal stamping plant. Plainly sociable by nature, he said he wanted to change careers to something that would allow him to meet more people.

Frank quizzed him about his knowledge of HVAC equipment and installation. Jack knew the subject, concisely summarizing the relative merits of forced-air versus low-pressure boiler systems, and recounting several ingenious solutions he'd implemented to keep his present employer's antiquated systems working optimally. He also modestly described how he had recently installed a new furnace in his own home. Jack particularly impressed Frank with his knowledge of new digital controllers and their operating efficiencies. On a personal level, Jack mentioned that he had three young boys and frequently volunteered at their Little League games and scouting events. Only his relationship with God, Jack said earnestly, was more important than his family.

After the interview, Frank personally called Jack's former employers for a reference. Each company confirmed Jack's prior employment but refused to provide further information, citing "company policy" as the reason. Pursuant to Jack's request, Frank did not contact his current employer, who Jack said would be upset to learn he was leaving and likely would say unkind things about him in retaliation. The next day, Frank went through the motions interviewing another applicant, an older man with considerable HVAC experience but with the personality of a gerbil. He later called Jack and offered him a job with a $2,000 per month base salary and generous commissions on sales. Jack enthusiastically accepted the offer. They agreed on a starting date and discussed Frank's ambitious sales goals. Just before hanging up, Jack said, "God bless you, boss. I won't let you down." Though not particularly religious himself, Frank found his words comforting.

During his first weeks with the company, Jack impressed everyone with his enthusiasm and initiative. Each morning, he'd pore over manuals and price lists, quickly becoming knowledgeable about every aspect of the HVAC business. He quizzed Frank extensively about current customers and suppliers, asking who had the lowest prices and best inventory. Jack also spent time on job sites to learn more about project management and systems installation. But despite his energy and willingness to learn, Jack failed to make a single sale during his first three weeks on the job.

Frank became completely fed up after another week went by without a sale. At a Monday morning staff meeting, he roughly interrogated Jack about his current prospects. The big man looked sheepishly at his small boss, a man half his size, who berated him for his "lousy" performance. Turning beet-red, Jack tried to reassure Frank that his leads would soon become sales and asked him to be patient. Frank rudely interrupted him, saying he didn't want excuses, he wanted results, gruffly adding that Jack would find his "sorry ass" on the unemployment line if he didn't turn it around soon. Several workers snickered while their feisty boss delivered his verbal whipping. Clenching and unclenching his fists, Jack Stoker darkly glared at his boss as the meeting moved on to scheduling matters. Later that day, several employees saw Jack fervently praying in the semiprivacy of the company lunchroom.

Jack eventually made a few small sales, but nothing of consequence. He also began spending more time out of the office supposedly making sales calls. However, he became inexplicably difficult to reach on his cellular phone and often took hours to respond to his pager.

As a congenital overachiever, Frank simply could not stomach someone who didn't carry his weight. At the end of two months, Frank gave up on Jack and decided to cut him loose. On a Friday afternoon, he bluntly told Jack he was letting him go effective immediately. Jack became emotional and begged for two more weeks to turn it around, blubbering that his family would be devastated if he were fired. Unnerved by the sight of a grown man crying, Frank reluctantly agreed to keep him on the payroll for an additional two weeks, after which he'd be laid off rather than fired, making him eligible for unemployment benefits while looking for a new job. Still snuffling, Jack raised his eyes upwards as if entreating the heavens to intervene in his hour of need. Then he dropped to his knees and asked Frank to pray with him. Astonished, Frank quickly declined and left the room, while Jack loudly asked the Lord for strength and comfort.

Over the next two weeks, Frank never once saw Jack, whose sales did not improve at all, confirming that letting him go was indeed the right decision. On the afternoon before Jack's last day, Frank was searching the supply room for an odd-sized thermocouple when he discovered Jack sprawled unconscious on the concrete floor. His eyes were rolled back and blood trickled from a tiny cut on his forehead. Though it was never confirmed, Jack apparently had bumped his head on a metal shelf at the end of an aisle formed by two storage racks. There was no conceivable reason for Jack to have been in that area. Unable to revive him, Frank called 911 and urgently requested an ambulance. Still unconscious when EMS arrived ten minutes later, Jack was rushed to the hospital, where he was revived. He spent the next two days undergoing a series of inconclusive neurological tests. With no memory whatsoever of his accident, Jack complained of a severe headache, dizziness, and a persistent ringing in his ears.

The week after his injury, Jack filed for workers' compensation benefits including disability income and reimbursement for medical expenses arising from his injury. Despite numerous tests and medical examinations, Jack's condition remained undiagnosed and untreated. Over the next six months, he showed no improvement whatsoever. In fact, he claimed to be growing worse with new complaints of depression, cognitive difficulties, and general physical malaise. Even getting out of bed in the morning, he told his doctor, had become unbearable. Jack hired a lawyer to represent his workers' compensation claim for permanent disability.

Excelsior Heating and Cooling Company, until Jack's accident, had maintained a positive account balance with the State Bureau of Workers' Compensation, entitling the firm to a preferential insurance rate.

Soon, the positive balance was gone because of Jack's claim and the company found itself in a "penalty rate" category, with coverage costing $12 for every $100 of payroll, quadruple the amount previously paid. Company profits went down significantly as a consequence. No one from Excelsior bothered to contact Jack Stoker or his family after his mysterious accident. The company, however, did receive periodic reports from the claims administrator that Frank was physically and emotionally incapacitated.

About a year after his injury, one of Excelsior's employees happened to observe Jack coaching a Little League game, seemingly fine other than becoming overwrought after a contested play at home plate. When told, Frank went totally ballistic in front of several employees, repeatedly punching a metal locker while spitting forth obscenities. To him, nothing was more contemptible than a malingerer, particularly one who was costing him considerable money. Still hyperventilating with rage, Frank called his attorney who calmly suggested an investigation.

Investigation and Aftermath

A review of the records at the State Bureau of Workers' Compensation revealed that Jack had made two questionable prior claims. One involved an "ear and head injury" from a minor explosion that had occurred while he was working for a natural gas company six years earlier. Though well away from the explosion and presenting no obvious injuries, Jack had gone to the emergency room the next day complaining of blackouts, a severe headache, and loss of hearing in his left ear. After collecting disability income for almost two years and being fitted with a hearing aid, he settled his claim for "permanent partial disability" for a lump-sum payment. His second prior claim was for a "soft tissue" back injury sustained while lifting an acetylene tank into a pickup truck. He received physical therapy, a back brace, occupational retraining in HVAC systems, and another settlement payment for "permanent partial disability" just weeks before being hired by Excelsior Heating & Cooling Company. While with Excelsior, Jack wore neither a back brace nor a hearing aid and never appeared disabled in any way. The attorney representing his claim against Excelsior had also handled his two prior cases.

A litigation search also turned up a civil suit arising from an automobile accident in which Jack had been rear-ended in stop-and-go traffic. Jack claimed he had suffered "severe whiplash," though his car had sustained no damage whatsoever. Jack's same attorney settled the case for $6,000 just before trial. Jack revealed this accident to a claims examiner in response to a question regarding previous injuries, saying his car had been "demolished" in the collision, which had rendered him unconscious. He never mentioned his "injuries" from the pipeline explosion.

The investigation quickly uncovered other suspicious information. A search of the secretary of state's records turned up a company, the Hot 'n Cold Corporation, having the same address as Jack's personal residence. According to the corporate filings, Jack's eighty-year-old mother was "statutory agent" and his wife was "president" of the company, which was formed about six months *before* Jack had been hired by Excelsior. Further checking revealed that the Hot 'n Cold Corporation had rented office space in a nearby suburb a month *after* Jack's injury. When located and questioned, the owner of the building disclosed that Jack Stoker had leased a small office for a very short time from which he ran "his HVAC contracting business," adding that "Jack handled sales but subcontracted out the installations to several young men working as independent contractors." The building owner also told the investigator he feared Jack and questioned his sanity after seeing him point a gun at a disgruntled subcontractor. The man cancelled Jack's month-to-month lease shortly thereafter, because, in his words, "my peace of mind is more important than money."

The investigator then tracked down the subcontractor, who despised Jack for "stiffing" him on an installation. Besides confirming the gun-pointing incident, the young man also described the Hot 'n Cold Corporation's business in some detail, even identifying several small jobs he'd done for Jack while he was supposedly working for Excelsior. When Jack first got started, the young man said, he couldn't make ends meet, necessitating his taking the job with Excelsior. Jack's business, however, had really taken off in the last few months after Hot 'n Cold landed a contract for a multi-unit residential development in an outlying area. Apparently, Jack operated the business by himself. His mother, the company's "statutory agent," lived in a nursing home in another state, and his wife, the "president," worked as a full-time waitress at a local steak house.

Further investigation confirmed that the Hot 'n Cold Corporation had done substantial business in the last year and maintained accounts with several suppliers. As the only apparent employee, Jack made the sales and supervised the work. Numerous written documents—including supplier credit applications, permit applications, construction contracts, contractor registration forms, business cards, and advertisements—linked Jack to the Hot 'n Cold Corporation. Among the documents found during the investigation was a Construction Industry Examining Board test application, which required the signatory to attest *under oath* all relevant work experience. Jack had sworn before a notary that he had worked "full time" for over a year as Hot 'n Cold's "CEO, secretary, manager and treasurer." Several general contractors provided sworn affidavits confirming that Jack had sold them HVAC systems and supervised the installations. An equipment supplier provided photocopies of the invoices for the furnaces installed on these projects with delivery acknowledged in writing by Jack Stoker.

Excelsior's lawyer, convinced there was clear and convincing evidence of fraud, presented his case at a hearing before the State Industrial Commission reviewing Jack's claim for "permanent partial disability." The attorney called the investigator, who testified for over an hour, describing his findings and introducing various documents and affidavits into evidence. Jack, who had shuffled into the hearing room seemingly dazed and confused, watched grimly from the corner of his eye. After company counsel had completed his questioning, Jack's attorney sprang up and accused the investigator of bias, questioned his credentials, and attacked his conclusions as "unsubstantiated." When pressured, the investigator acknowledged that he had never spoken with Jack and had never seen him actually perform any work.

The investigator also admitted that he did not know if Jack *personally* earned any income while collecting workers' compensation benefits. He could only confirm that the company had income during that time.

In an Oscar-worthy performance, Jack then testified in a frail and trembling voice that he had "helped out" his "wife's company" on his "better days." His wife, he testified, made all the decisions and managed every aspect of the business. When asked on cross-examination how his wife found time to run an HVAC business while working full-time as a waitress, he responded that she was a "brilliant woman," adding that he hoped she'd hire him if he ever recovered from his mysterious ailment. Jack further testified that he "never received a dime" for helping out. His wife, however, received a regular paycheck and an occasional dividend from company profits. When Excelsior's counsel pressed him about his being the sole signatory for the company checking account, Jack testified that he wrote the checks because gripping a pen aggravated his wife's arthritis. As a caring husband, it was his "duty" to spare her this discomfort.

Following the hearing, Excelsior's attorney turned over the investigative results to the Special Investigations Unit of the Bureau of Workers' Compensation. Without any further inquiry, without even questioning Jack Stoker, the fraud unit determined that it could not prove "intent" to commit fraud and therefore issued a finding of "no probable cause." Jack continued receiving full benefits.

On the advice of legal counsel, Frank Rickmann eventually agreed to a $50,000 settlement some weeks later to cap Excelsior's exposure, and the Bureau of Workers' Compensation approved the deal. Frank ultimately paid many thousands of dollars in higher premiums because of Jack Stoker's claim. Though there was indisputable evidence that Jack had been soliciting for a competitor while employed by Excelsior, without an employment or a noncompete agreement, Excelsior had no basis for a lawsuit against Jack. Its sole recourse was firing him.

Frank Rickmann was a changed man after the experience. Though tightly wound and demanding beforehand, Frank thereafter became an angry tyrant, easily provoked and impossibly impatient with his employees. The company's special *esprit de corps* evaporated, replaced by a poisonous work environment where everyone felt put-upon. Within a year, Excelsior's two lead men quit to go into business for themselves, which Frank took as another personal betrayal.

After receiving his disability settlement, Jack Stoker worked openly for the Hot 'n Cold Corporation until the company filed for bankruptcy protection about a year later. Several subcontractors and suppliers went unpaid, experiencing combined losses in the low six figures. Jack moved from the area without leaving a forwarding address, though rumors circulated that he'd moved his family to Florida to open another HVAC contracting business in a rapidly growing retirement community.

□ □ □ **COMMENTARY AND ANALYSIS**

When it comes to evaluating people, a sound credo is to follow your gut feeling when it is bad, and to ignore your gut feeling when it is good. Frauds and con artists generally make a dazzling first impression, appearing much the way fool's gold does to a prospector. They look at first like the "real thing" but never hold up under close inspection. Unfortunately, their true character generally becomes evident only after they inflict pain and disappointment. Frank Rickmann made the classic mistake of trusting his first impression when he hired Jack Stoker, oblivious to the fact that someone friendly and outgoing may not be ethical and trustworthy. Ironically, employers should be particularly cautious when interviewing likable job applicants. Charm and sociability tend to impair interviewers' objectivity, leading to costly lapses in judgment.

Frank further dropped his guard when Jack Stoker conspicuously revealed his religiosity during his job interview. This should have made Frank suspicious. Truly devout people will normally keep their spirituality to themselves when meeting someone for the first time. Frauds will often feign religiosity in the effort to establish trust with the unsuspecting. Jack's loudly proclaiming his personal devotion to God should have been a tip-off that the man warranted close scrutiny before being hired.

But even without checking out Jack's background and prior work history, Frank probably could have eliminated Jack from consideration during his first interview. It is worth repeating that applicants with problematic pasts will usually withdraw themselves from consideration if employers follow certain steps during the hiring process. At their initial meeting, Frank should have advised Jack clearly and unambiguously that all job applicants are thoroughly investigated prior to being hired, and are also required to pass a drug and alcohol test following a job offer as a condition of employment. Frank then should have emphatically added that the pre-employment investigation would include detailed discussions with Jack's prior supervisors, whose names and addresses must be provided on the application form. After these disclosures, Frank should then have pointed out the clause on the application form stating that inaccuracies, omissions, misinformation, or dishonesty of any kind will result in rejection or immediate dismissal if detected after being hired. If employers rigorously follow these steps at the very first meeting, most con artists and frauds will not finish the application process, much like burglars who shun houses with security signs prominently posted out front. When an applicant abruptly withdraws, offering only a feeble explanation if one at all, employers should take comfort knowing they have been saved the aggravation of assessing someone unfit for the job opening.

But what more could Frank have been done? After all, he contacted Jack's former employers and obtained no useful information other than verification of prior employment. For starters, Frank should have tried harder to get detailed information concerning Jack's competency, work ethic, and reliability. Getting this kind of information can be a challenge. Other than confirming dates of employment, many corporations will reveal almost nothing about former employees, hewing to a practice much like the strict military code of giving only name, rank, and serial number under the rules of war. Cowed by the possibility of litigation, increasing numbers of companies adopt this defensive posture in the misguided belief that a less than positive reference can lead to grave legal consequences. In reality, an employer may be just as exposed to liability by saying nothing to a prospective new employer about a former employee, particularly if that former employee has a history of aggression, negligence, harassing behavior, or drug and alcohol abuse. "Negligent failure to warn" lawsuits have become increasingly prevalent in recent years.

Simply verifying prior employment, despite its insufficiency, certainly does have some value when evaluating the worthiness of a job applicant. If the check reveals that an individual has blatantly lied in some material way, such as the supposed "marketing director" who actually worked as a salesman, the investigation can end right there. The applicant should automatically be eliminated from further consideration as untrustworthy. If the verification check, however, confirms the applicant's representations in regard to past employment, additional information might also be provided that can be helpful.

Before contacting Jack's previous employers, Frank should have obtained from Jack a signed "release and authorization," something discussed last chapter, allowing a comprehensive background investigation. This release should have included a broadly worded "indemnification and hold-harmless" clause absolving prior employers from any and all liability for providing an honest reference. Jack's previous employers might have been more cooperative had they been provided a copy of this signed document. Frank also could have reassured them that any information provided would be kept confidential—unsuccessful candidates would be told only that someone else was hired, without further explanation. If the former employers continued to balk, Frank could then have offered to modify the release and authorization to address any additional concerns. With friendly persistence, most companies can be persuaded into giving some kind of appraisal of an applicant.

Former employers who still refuse to provide information can be further pressured by being told that the job applicant cannot be hired without honest and detailed assessments of prior work history. Frank Rickmann should have told Jack's former employers that their refusal to provide a reference would be conveyed to Jack in writing as the reason for his being eliminated from consideration. They then would be in the uncomfortable position of derailing Jack's employment opportunity, possibly becoming liable for damages, ironically in the misguided effort to avoid liability by saying nothing. Persistent, incremental pressure can usually induce the most reticent references to become more talkative.

Very large corporations, however, are largely indifferent to pressure and will steadfastly adhere to a policy of providing nothing other than confirmation of prior employment. These same large corporations, however, almost always maintain extensive personnel records including written performance reviews, disciplinary actions, and other information related to job performance. Under many collective bargaining agreements and state employment laws, employees (and former employees) are entitled to copies of their personnel files upon written request. After being rebuffed by Jack's prior employers, Frank Rickmann should have asked Jack to sign letters addressed to his former employers requesting copies of his personnel files, including all performance reviews, commendations, attendance records, and documentation concerning any disciplinary actions taken against him. The request should also have included an oversized, postage-paid return envelope addressed to Jack in care of the business offices of Excelsior Heating and Cooling. Needless to say, Jack would never have signed these letters, knowing his poor employment record would likely have been revealed had he done so. Instead of signing, Jack likely would have withdrawn his application.

Obtaining a thorough and candid assessment of an applicant's capabilities and character should be the primary goal when contacting prior employers. This requires speaking with the people most familiar with an applicant, such as a former supervisor or close work associate, who are well qualified to comment on an applicant's competency and work ethic. A good way to identify and locate such people is to shift the responsibility for doing so to the applicant. Frank should have asked Jack to provide the names, *home* addresses, and telephone numbers of his former supervisors. When they are contacted at home, former supervisors almost always yield a more open and candid appraisal of a former employee. Applicants with a problematic past, however, will almost always claim that they cannot get this information for any number of reasons. Qualified applicants, on the other hand, will go to great lengths to locate people able to verify their superior work history.

In this case, Jack would have furnished neither the names nor the addresses of his prior supervisors, knowing they would likely give him scathing appraisals. Jack would have instead given excuses, such as saying his former supervisors had all retired, moved away, or otherwise become unavailable. If Frank had pressed him for at least their names, Jack would have waffled and stammered something nonsensical. Careful, patient, persistent, and probing questions will eventually elicit absurd responses from all fraudsters. Even accomplished fakers like Jack Stoker are incapable of fabricating a detailed and plausible falsified history on the fly, complete with the full names and titles of supervisors, job assignments, and work responsibilities. When pressed for specific information, people like Jack often become forgetful, remembering only first names and answering in vague generalities. They will falter and stammer as they struggle to get their story straight. Always listen for pauses! Whenever you hear three "uhs" strung together, know that whatever follows in such situations is likely to be a lie. On the other hand, people with nothing to hide can recite without hesitation the names of every supervisor and job responsibility, often going back decades.

In addition to names, employers should always press applicants for their former supervisors' job titles, the duration and extent of their supervisory functions, and the applicant's thoughts on their former supervisors' ability or willingness to provide fair and objective assessments of their prior work performance. Employers should listen very carefully to their responses, looking for evidence of evasiveness, hostility, or unusual anxiety. An applicant's disclosures concerning previous problems with supervisors should not automatically cause alarm. Just about everyone has clashed with a manager at least once in the past. But upright people with clean consciences are generally up-front about their frictions and conflicts with others. Those with disgraceful pasts, however, are likely to squirm, censure, criticize, turn red, and then spew forth accusatory tales about how they've been previously victimized, misunderstood, or underappreciated. Polite but persistent probing for specifics will generally expose this kind of behavior from troublemakers.

Employers should even consider asking applicants to contact former supervisors to arrange a personal reference and interview. Those candidates who fail to locate and speak with their former supervisors may have something to hide or may simply lack drive and initiative, each cause for concern. When a candidate succeeds in making arrangements, however, former supervisors will generally speak honestly and frankly, particularly on behalf of superior individuals. When contacted, the former supervisor should always be reminded that the applicant provided his or her name as a *personal* reference. The most valuable and informative references, after all, come from people, not companies. By seeing themselves as a personal reference, not a company reference, former supervisors will speak more freely.

As an audacious conniver, Jack might well have provided bogus references had Frank asked him to make such arrangements. Unethical yet enterprising applicants like Jack occasionally furnish fraudulent references in an attempt to hide a troubled past or improve upon a lackluster work history. The internet has spawned a number of disreputable entrepreneurs who specialize in providing this "service." Asking detailed questions about the company and the applicant, however, easily exposes these charlatans. If a reference seems hurried, sounds cagey, speaks in vague or meaningless generalities, or otherwise raises suspicions, always ask the reference to confirm something you know to be false. For example, if the applicant has represented on his application that he previously worked two years as a quality inspector, ask the reference to confirm that the applicant worked five years as a dispatcher. Authentic references will instantly correct the error. You can then follow up by saying, "Oh yes, my mistake! I was confusing the applicant with someone else under consideration." It is always a good idea to call the reference at work for a "follow-up question." If the company has never heard of the person, or if the reference sounds noticeably different and has no recollection of the previous conversation, obviously there is a problem.

Of course, Jack's disability claims and his abuse of the workers compensation system were the most alarming aspects of his prior work history. Had Frank known about them beforehand, he certainly would not have hired Jack. Obtaining and acting on this information, however, could have had serious legal consequences under the Americans with Disabilities Act (ADA). Among the provisions of this Act, employers are strictly prohibited from inquiring about an applicant's medical condition and physical handicaps until after an offer of employment has been made. Asking Jack beforehand if there was anything that might affect his ability to do the job would have been legally permissible. Asking anything further in regard to his medical history would have been a violation of the law. Similarly, checking Jack's claims history prior to a job offer would have been simply asking for trouble considering Jack's litigious nature. Faced with these legal obstacles, speaking candidly with Jack's prior supervisors was all the more important, since they likely would have volunteered this information. Of course, under a strict interpretation of the law, Frank should not have eliminated Jack from consideration because of his suspicious injury claims. Nothing would have prohibited Frank, however, from continuing his search for someone better qualified for the sales position.

An almost surefire way Jack could have been eliminated from consideration, even in the absence of candid appraisals from supervisors, would have been for Frank to offer him a job and then ask about any prior work-related claims and injuries. Jack almost certainly would have concealed his prior claims, particularly since he had ceased his charade of wearing his back brace and hearing aid. Thereafter, Frank would have been legally entitled to review Jack's records at the Bureau of Workers' Compensation, which of course would have revealed an entirely different story. Frank could then have rescinded the job offer—not for Jack's prior medical history, but instead for "inaccuracies, omissions, misinformation, or dishonesty," reasons identified in the application as justifiable causes for rejection or dismissal if detected after being hired.

Frank's failure to evaluate Jack's past was attributable in part to his positive first impression of the man. After a great interview with a charismatic applicant, most employers understandably expect a background investigation to confirm that the applicant is the right person for the job, not the wrong one. This is a dangerous mindset, leaving them vulnerable to a major mistake. Many charismatic applicants reach their highest level of competence during their job interview, and later disappoint in actual job performance. Vigilance and sound judgment require that positive feelings should always be ignored when hiring someone new. A pre-employment investigation should begin with the assumption that there is something disqualifying in every applicant's past and the goal should be to find it. Instead of expecting a favorable finding, an employer should expect the opposite, and then be pleasantly surprised when nothing unfavorable is uncovered. Had Frank done this, he would never have hired someone with such a problematic past.

Preventing Fraud

Frank's failings, of course, went far beyond the inadequate way he checked out Jack's past before hiring him. Like all victims of fraud, Frank was complicit by providing Jack the opportunity to commit fraud. Frank's lax supervision, which was nothing less than negligent, gave Jack ample room to work for himself while on Excelsior's payroll. Jack's accepting a paycheck may have been the equivalent of stealing, but Frank's failure to monitor Jack was comparable to leaving his company's cash receipts unsecured and untended. Should we truly feel sorry for the victim who leaves money on a windowsill and later finds it missing? Experience shows that opportunities for fraud *will* eventually be exploited, and those who create the opportunities share responsibility when the fraud finally occurs.

Had Frank closely monitored Jack's activities and verified his sales presentations and travel itineraries, Jack's deceit would have been exposed much earlier. With close supervision, Jack might even have performed responsibly. Keep in mind that those who create the opportunity for fraud in effect create the temptation and thereby share culpability when fraud finally happens. In business, sins of commission often ensue from sins of omission. In a very real sense, Frank Rickmann was as much to blame as Jack for the problems that befell him and his company.

In addition to "opportunity," one of the essential elements of every fraud is "rationalization." Perpetrators always rationalize their misdeeds as either justified or excusable. For example, embezzlers may begin by telling themselves they are only "borrowing" the money, not stealing it, fully intending to pay it back someday. Of course they never do. Another common rationalization is that misconduct is appropriate and justifiable revenge for a perceived offense, the "eye for an eye" excuse. Besides giving Jack the opportunity, Frank also gave him reason to commit fraud by publicly humiliating him at the staff meeting. Employers and supervisors should never censure or embarrass subordinates publicly. Criticism should instead be conveyed in private, without emotion, and always directed toward the behavior and not the person. Insults, particularly public ones, tend to trigger the impulse to get even, and subsequent misdeeds will be rationalized away by the perpetrators as fully warranted.

Frank gave Jack further cause for seeking revenge by firing him. Today, many employees—even incompetent ones—tend to look upon their jobs not as a privilege but as an entitlement. People perceive being fired as equivalent to being robbed. Rarely do fired workers believe they deserved to be fired. If anything, they believe they deserved another chance. Call it denial or delusion, but a great many people are simply incapable of admitting responsibility for their own failings. In America today, it seems someone else is always at fault.

As cruel as it may appear, problem employees like Jack should be fired immediately and quietly escorted to the door. No possible good can come from giving an employee notice of impending discharge. No matter how employers try to soften the blow through severance packages and kind words, some employees will take offense and many will try to get even. Jack likely felt resentful, not thankful, when Frank compassionately gave him more time to turn it around. Unfortunately, in doing so Frank also gave Jack the opportunity to implement his more serious and more costly fraud, faking a workplace injury. Employers should remember that providing notice and severance benefits may make them feel better, but those things don't always make the fired employees feel better. Discharged employees almost always walk away unhappy to some degree.

Frank's tangible losses from his disastrous selection of Jack as his sales representative can only partially be calculated in bottom-line financial terms. Money paid to Jack in salary was a complete waste, a direct hit to the company's bottom line. But that loss was nothing in comparison to the financial blow of significantly higher workers' compensation insurance premiums. Had Frank absorbed the first loss but avoided the second, he would undoubtedly have sidestepped the intangible costs—the distrust, discord, and emotional pain—that were ultimately more hurtful than his financial setbacks. Peace of mind, Frank would be the first to attest, is always more important than money.

Today, employers frequently have their peace of mind undermined by employee mischief that often seems as though it's protected or even made possible by government regulation. Jack's staged mishap was an inspired though devious way to keep his paychecks coming, and one entirely supported by state statutes and regulations. Under current workers' compensation laws, if a claim has even the slightest basis in fact it generally will be allowed. The system almost always gives the injured employee the benefit of the doubt; the burden falls to the employer to prove that a disability claim should be denied. The fact that Jack was injured on the job almost guaranteed that he would be covered and compensated. The only question really was how much he would receive in compensation.

Make no mistake: the majority of disability claims filed every year are legitimate, often the consequence of unsafe workplace conditions and practices that are, on the whole, more reprehensible than all the frauds perpetrated on the system. Employers have a duty, both morally and legally, to provide a safe and healthy work environment. That said, workers' compensation fraud and abuse is a growing and costly problem in America today. Many employees filing claims consider the benefits to be akin to an enhanced earnings package or vacation time, as something owed for prior performance. For Jack, his disability claim served as a financial safety net providing income for over a year, with the tab ultimately paid by Frank through higher premiums.

In a very real sense, Frank's lax response allowed the fraud to continue. He could have unmasked Jack's deception by periodically checking in on him after his "injury." It is always a good idea to keep in close contact with injured workers, whether you're motivated primarily by concern or by distrust. Fraudulent injuries and malingering can easily be exposed by unscheduled visits to check in on purportedly injured workers. There is nothing inherently offensive about this kind of contact; after all, the neighborly delivery of a chicken casserole for the house-bound is always well received by those truly ailing. Frank, however, neglected to monitor Jack's recovery and thereby unwittingly ensured that Jack's disability payments continued unabated.

After finally learning he had been bamboozled, Frank's emotions devolved into near derangement when it became obvious that the "system" offered him no justice and no equitable relief. Frank learned firsthand that employers should never take it for granted that a regulatory agency can rectify a wrong. From my experience as an investigator, I have come to believe that government regulators dash hopes as often or more than they realize them. Few things are more demoralizing than first being victimized and then seeing the authorities do nothing about it. Most of us have chuckled over the observation that it is always a lie when someone says, "I'm from the government and I'm here to help you." Those who experience this firsthand, however, never find it funny. Jack's transgressions were less vexing to Frank than the government's failure to investigate and prosecute what he felt was a clear case of criminal fraud. It was an outrageous miscarriage of justice that will color Frank's outlook on life forever. All too often, regulators and prosecutors seem to look for reasons *not* to go after the bad guys, perhaps from fear of failure, crushing caseloads, or simply out of laziness. In this case, the fraud unit's assertion that it could not "prove" intent was nothing less than a cop-out. With the government failing to punish such mischief, employers must watch out for themselves and be especially careful about who they bring into their organizations. Mistakes can have serious and long-lasting consequences. Frank's ordeal continues unabated, and should serve as a lesson to us all.

□ □ □ **CAUTIONARY TIPS:**

- Be suspicious of people who make a conspicuous show of their religious devotion at first meeting. Scoundrels often pretend to be devout to establish trust.

- When conducting a pre-employment background investigation, assume there is negative information to be found that will disqualify an applicant. Then doggedly search for it.

- Never censure or criticize people publicly. Bad employees often will rationalize misdeeds as justifiable retaliation for an affront. Many will try to "get even" with an employer they feel has wronged or humiliated them.

- Problem employees should be fired immediately and escorted to the door. No possible good can come from giving an employee notice of impending discharge. No matter how you try to soften the blow through severance packages and kind words, discharged employees will experience some measure of disgruntlement, and some will feel justified to "get even."

- Never take it for granted that a government regulatory agency can or will rectify a wrong.

- Always keep in touch with injured workers. Fraudulent injuries and malingering can easily be exposed with unscheduled contact.

CHAPTER 5

Intentional Torts/Workplace Accidents

□ □ □ **CASE #1—HARLAN HUGHES:**
   "OUR SAFETY PROGRAM? I TOLD THEM TO BE CAREFUL."

Not a day went by without Harlan Hughes regretting he'd purchased that damned oil field just months before the Persian Gulf War in 1991. At the time, he'd thought it a brilliant move—oil prices were approaching historic highs, buoyed by worldwide anxiety about the impending conflict. Things did not work out as he'd anticipated. Harlan had planned to hold the property for less than a year and then flip it at a big profit after oil prices soared during a protracted, disruptive war with Iraq. Who would have guessed that the coalition troops would blow through the vaunted Iraqi military so easily? Instead of soaring, oil prices dropped like a stone within days of Kuwait's liberation. Instead of a lucrative investment, his purchase of eighty-six mostly depleted oil wells turned out to be a financial fiasco for Harlan Hughes and his family partners. In truth, Prosperity Oil Inc. could not have been a more unfitting name for his company. It was certain never to recoup the money he'd invested, barring the outbreak of World War III.

One of the cruel jokes of nature is that oil wells become more costly to operate at the end of their economic lives, financially squeezing operators with declining production revenues and rising operating expenses. As well pressures drop, paraffin often precipitates and accumulates down-hole, plugging tubing perforations and gumming up sucker rods, which in turn slows oil flow and strains pumpjack motors that must work doubly hard for less and less production. Untreated wells can develop serious operating problems: rods seize and break, motors burn out, and producing formations eventually seal off. When such cascading problems occur, an older well has little hope of making money again for the unlucky operator.

With his oil field now decades old, Harlan Hughes had paraffin problems with more than half the wells, and the cost of treating them was getting more expensive every month. For some years, Harlan had hired a contractor to treat the wells with toluene, which was delivered by a small tanker truck on a regularly scheduled basis. A highly volatile chemical, toluene is used today mostly as an additive to increase the octane of gasoline; it's also as an essential solvent in glues and paints. Toluene is used in the oil patch because it dissolves paraffin as easily as sugar in water. A known health hazard, overexposure to the chemical has been linked to liver cancer and neurological problems in humans. Harlan Hughes, however, knew little about toluene other than that he needed it to keep his wells operating, but couldn't afford it at the prices he'd been paying the contractor. This dilemma impelled him to buy at auction an old, one-ton tanker truck previously used by a lawn-care company. He also made arrangements to buy toluene in bulk. Harlan reasoned that his "pumpers"—the employees who worked the field—could treat the wells themselves at a fraction of the costs he'd been paying.

At an early morning field meeting, Harlan disclosed his money-saving scheme to his pumpers and outlined their new responsibilities. What Harlan said that morning would later be used against him during the ensuing wrongful-death lawsuit as evidence of his intentional disregard for the health and safety of his workers. From Harlan's point of view, however, he'd only been trying to preserve the company and his workers' jobs, trying to keep food on their tables. Cutting costs, in his mind, was a responsible demonstration of his concern for their personal welfare in addition to the financial welfare of the company. Unfortunately, there is often a disconnect between intentions and impressions, as demonstrated by how Harlan's words were later remembered in depositions.

The able men who work the Appalachian oil patch may not have much formal education, but they have refined antennae for what they consider bullshit, and that is precisely how they interpreted Harlan's remarks that chilly morning. Harlan gave a short speech about the growing financial problems of the company, how all their jobs (including his own) were at risk, how their obligations to "the company shareholders" (i.e. Harlan and the Hughes family) required greater efforts and cost-cutting measures, and how more would be expected of them in the future. He then informed them that henceforth they'd be responsible for treating the wells themselves, and that toluene would be purchased in bulk and stored in an empty 210-barrel tank connected to an idle well that hadn't produced in years. There would be no additional compensation for this work, he added with emphasis, as if reading their collective minds.

Without knowing the specific risks, the pumpers all knew that toluene was a hazardous substance, a highly explosive liquid that required careful handling. For years they'd watched the contractor who treated their wells with toluene, always wearing a respirator, impervious gloves, and eye protection. He'd unfailingly made the pumpers stand clear and repeatedly warned them about the dangers of breathing the vapors. An older pumper named Bearcat Borden, a capable but not a particularly articulate man, haltingly asked if they'd be provided any safety gear and training in the proper handling of toluene. Harlan, utterly unknowledgeable in practical oil-field matters, mistakenly thought Bearcat was joking with him, rather than expressing sincere concern about a serious issue.

"Here's what you do, men," replied Harlan, grinning and bobbing his eyebrows like Groucho. "Don't smoke butts when you work with toluene or you might singe your whiskers; remember to hold your breath when you're around the stuff; and for all you glue-sniffers, please refrain from recreational use while on company time. What you do on your own time is none of my business."

Unused to irony, none of the pumpers smiled let alone laughed, and Harlan instantly felt self-conscious and disconnected from his blue-collar employees. He incorrectly interpreted their reticence as insolence and derision. His facetious, light-hearted tone changed in a heartbeat.

"Look, I'm giving you an assignment and I expect you to do it," he said firmly. "If you want to keep your jobs, you'll treat the wells, and keep them pumping. Production is down, income is down . . . I want improvement within a month."

Bearcat, a compulsive rule-follower since his days in the military, innocently asked if the township allowed the storage of toluene. "Don't we need a license or an EPA permit or something? You know, toluene is dangerous stuff."

"I'll worry about that," snapped Harlan, just before ending the meeting and stalking off to his new Lexus. "Just keep quiet about the toluene. There's no danger if you're careful . . . there isn't even a farmhouse within a quarter mile. Besides, what the township officials don't know won't hurt them."

About six weeks later, an anxious Bearcat Borden went looking for Benny Weed, the youngest pumper on staff, who'd failed to return home for dinner. Benny's wife Ginny had called him in a panic after her husband, then more than two hours late, failed to answer his cell phone despite her repeated attempts to reach him. As the low man on the company totem pole, Benny generally got stuck with treating the wells with toluene, something he usually did late in the day after tending the wells assigned to him. On a hunch, Bearcat went straight to the toluene storage tank and found Benny crumpled unconscious beside it, still breathing but with his head split and oozing, his scalp matted with blood. In an instant, he scooped up the young man, loaded him into his truck, and raced him to the nearest hospital, thirty miles away. Despite intense medical efforts to save him, Benny Weed died just after midnight from a severely fractured skull.

Investigation and Aftermath

The coroner's perfunctory inquiry, typical of many rural counties, ruled that Benny Weed had died accidentally, having apparently fallen backwards from an access ladder welded to the oil storage tank. A deputy sheriff had briefly interviewed Bearcat Borden, who verified how he'd found the injured man and rushed him to the hospital. No one else was interviewed. Ginny Weed and her two young children were later granted a workers' compensation accidental-death payment of $20,000 and Social Security support of $928 per month.

Harlan Hughes called another early-morning field meeting shortly after the accident to share his sorrow over Benny's death and to try to rally the troops. His efforts failed miserably. Employees always doubt the sincerity of employers who express concerns and caring words only after the occurrence of something catastrophic. Employers who truly care about their workers make it known in hundreds of small ways long before something terrible happens. The pumpers listened silently as Harlan spewed clichés about "pulling together" and "moving on" and "celebrating" Benny's life through "an increased devotion to work." The pumpers felt as though Harlan had administered them a verbal dose of ipecac.

In truth, Harlan Hughes had been highly anxious since receiving news of Benny's death. Though the local authorities had quickly closed the case, Harlan suspected more bad things would surely come from the tragedy. At the very least, Prosperity Oil Inc. would be paying much higher premiums for its workers' compensation insurance, another serious blow to company finances.

"I've decided to have the toluene well-treatments contracted out again," said Harlan uncomfortably at the end of the field meeting. "We're already stretched thin with the unfortunate loss of Benny. You don't need more work at this difficult time, so I think we should forget about doing the treatments ourselves, at least for the time being. I need not remind you that the company is seriously strapped financially—any more losses and we may have to throw in the towel. The shareholders have talked about selling out if we cannot operate more efficiently, so just be careful what you do or say—after all, we sink or swim together."

Though delivered in a quiet, conspiratorial tone, Harlan's veiled threat was perfectly clear to the pumpers, who felt both scared and sickened. Beginning in the late 1980s, jobs in the oil patch had grown scarcer with each passing year. For most of them, oil roustabout work was all they knew. They fully understood, however, that their employer had essentially told them to keep their yaps shut about the toluene and Benny's death. As it turned out, one of them wouldn't cooperate.

Shortly thereafter, Ginny Weed received an anonymous, handwritten note that read, "Benny's accident needs more looking into. Ginny, hire you a lawyer." The note was signed, "A friend." Ginny took the letter to William Jeffries, an attorney who'd served with her on the pastor-parish relations committee at their church. Though they were from decidedly different sides of the tracks, Mr. Jeffries had always been gracious and respectful whenever he spoke with her. She had been intending to contact him for help with the death benefit applications and other legal issues. Receiving the anonymous note helped her shake off her grief-induced lethargy and call him.

At a meeting the next day, Mr. Jeffries agreed to help her obtain everything due her and her children, and also to look into the circumstances behind her husband's death. He had a calm, compassionate, reassuring manner, and for her sake kept to himself his suspicion that there was more to Benny's death than a simple "slip and fall" accident. He obtained the names and phone numbers of several of Benny's coworkers, one of whom undoubtedly wrote the note. After she left, he called and met with an investigator who had special training in accident investigations.

Bearcat Borden, the first person the investigator contacted, was initially reluctant to say anything other than to repeat what he'd previously told the deputy sheriff. The investigator, who'd interviewed hundreds of witnesses, sensed Bearcat was holding back—his twitchy body language and pained facial expression hinted at his distress and inner burdens. Patience and friendly empathy often help the more reticent open up. A few sociable beers helped Bearcat, too; after imbibing a few at the Hogshead Bar and Grill, Bearcat finally told the investigator about the tank of toluene, the absence of any training and safety measures, Harlan's implicit cover-up, and his own personal suspicions that Benny had been overcome by fumes after opening the manhole cover of the storage tank, causing him to fall backward from twelve feet up.

By interviewing Bearcat and several other employees, the investigator quickly identified many violations of OSHA's safety and health standards, including the company's failure to report Benny's death to the nearest OSHA office within eight hours as required by federal regulation. In fact, OSHA would probably never even have learned of the accident were it not for the investigator's call, which triggered an expedited OSHA investigation. Interviewed separately by the investigator, the pumpers each expressed anger with Harlan for his indifference to their health and safety. Each bitterly recalled his shocking comments regarding the "proper" handling of the toluene. One younger pumper even blamed Harlan for contributing to Benny's death by "putting ideas in his head."

This young pumper confidentially told the investigator that Benny may have been experimenting with "huffing," purposely breathing toluene vapors in order to get high. He knew for a fact that Benny had been a huffer in high school, which may have had something to do with his poor academic performance. Huffing involves inhaling intoxicating fumes from a variety of volatile products, an alarming practice that has become a silent epidemic among millions of mostly younger Americans. Benny Weed, his young colleague surmised, may have climbed the toluene tank to indulge in a magnum dose of toluene. Huffing toluene provides a euphoric rush that lasts about forty-five minutes, stimulating the same pleasure centers in the brain as cocaine. The pleasures of huffing, however, come at a terrible price. Breathing toluene vapor can cause organ damage, neurological and mental impairment, irritability, confusion, insomnia, irregular heartbeat, dizziness, and (as in Benny's case) loss of consciousness.

After the investigator notified OSHA about the events at Prosperity Oil Inc., the OSHA regional office called Harlan Hughes to inform him that an investigative team would arrive the next morning to look into the death of Benny Weed. Harlan quickly had the residual toluene drained from the tank and hauled to a disposal facility before they arrived, thinking OSHA would fine the company if toluene were found. Of course, OSHA already knew all about the toluene even before inspecting the scene of the accident. Harlan made it even worse for himself by first playing dumb and denying any knowledge of any toxic solvents or chemicals at the tank site where Benny had been fatally injured. His feckless cover-up quickly unraveled. With the help of the private investigator and some useful employee tips, the OSHA inspectors tracked the toluene to an injection well used mostly for the regulated disposal of brine and other oil field waste liquids.

The easiest, most cost-effective way to develop a winning civil lawsuit is to let the government regulators do the work for you. Attorney William Jeffries, already planning to file a wrongful death suit on behalf of Benny's estate, sat back and waited for OSHA to complete its work. Once involved, the OSHA regulators turned Prosperity Oil Inc. inside out, examining not simply Benny's death but every operational practice of the company. Just before OSHA released its findings in a final report, Harlan Hughes was stunned to learn from the OSHA regional director that the case would be referred to the Department of Justice for possible criminal indictment. He advised Harlan to retain an attorney.

OSHA ultimately cited Prosperity Oil Inc. for three "willful" violations (the gravest citations issued by the agency) of the Occupational Safety and Health Act (OSHAct), for improper handling of a known toxic substance, lying to inspectors, and obstructing an accident investigation. OSHA ascribes "willful" to those violations that an employer knowingly commits or commits with plain indifference to the law. In addition, OSHA cited Prosperity Oil Inc. for three "serious" violations, a classification assigned when "a substantial probability" of serious harm (or death) could result from the cited condition or practice, and when he employer knew, or should have known, of the hazard. Lastly, Prosperity Oil Inc. received citations for eighteen "other than serious violations," a laundry list of lesser OSHAct violations that included such things as inadequate record keeping and failure to post legally required warning signs.

The regional OSHA director fined the company a combined total of $112,687 for the violations. Though Harlan spent several sleep-deprived months waiting and worrying, criminal indictments were never brought against him or his company. The U.S. attorney, a man with political ambitions, had a loaded legal gun but wouldn't pull the trigger, deciding against prosecution because the odds of a criminal conviction were, in his mind, too uncertain.

Though Benny Weed's blood had been tested for the presence of alcohol and drugs after his death, no tests had been conducted for the presence of toluene. After OSHA's investigation, further tests indicated elevated concentrations of toluene in the blood samples they'd retained. With this new information, supported further by OSHA's well-documented findings and the incriminating information assembled by his own investigator, William Jeffries brought suit against Harlan Hughes and Prosperity Oil Inc. on behalf of the estate of Benny

Weed, Ginny Weed, and their young children for the "wrongful death" of Benny Weed, demanding a jury trial and seeking $5,000,000 in compensatory and punitive damages.

Filing a motion for summary judgment, Harlan Hughes's attorney asked the court to throw out the case before trial, arguing that by law, the workers' compensation system provided the "exclusive remedy" for workplace injuries, including deaths, thereby providing employers with immunity from tort liability. Ruling against Harlan Hughes and Prosperity Oil Inc., the court noted in its decision a judicially created exception to the Workers' Compensation Act for an "intentional tort"—any act committed with intent to cause, or that is substantially certain to cause, the injury or death of an employee. In his ruling, the judge declared there were "issues of fact" that had to be decided by a jury at trial.

Once the case was set for trial, settlement negotiations began in earnest. Harlan's attorney bluntly told his client that he had a high probability of losing; juries usually dispensed rough justice in cases that had strong emotional appeal, such as this one, with a grieving widow with young children facing a grim and uncertain future. At first, Harlan had trouble accepting his precarious legal position and, like many defendants facing bad legal outcomes, he attacked and berated his attorney for having failed him.

"I may have been stupid, maybe even negligent," argued Harlan vehemently. "But I never intentionally hurt anyone in my life. How can a jury possibly conclude that I intentionally tried to kill Benny Weed?"

Harlan's attorney patiently explained how juries often have trouble discerning the subtle difference between gross negligence and an intentional tort, often finding for the plaintiff on the basis that the injury or death was "substantially certain" to occur given the circumstances of the case. The sympathies of the jury would unquestionably be with the plaintiffs, not with some rich businessman trying to hide behind the Workers' Compensation Act to escape liability for his misdeeds.

Another important issue impelled Harlan to settle before trial. The company's insurance policy listed among its exceptions coverage for losses from "intentional acts." The policy obligated the insurance company to pay for his legal defense, but not for any ensuing adverse judgment. Like many businesspeople today, Harlan Hughes found himself caught up in a legal controversy in which the interests of his insurance company deviated from his own. Harlan had been surprised to learn his insurance company had no real incentive to win at trial. Unfortunately, he'd never bothered beforehand to read his insurance policy, which spelled out the exception in clear, unambiguous language.

As the trial approached, the attorneys from both sides cobbled together a settlement in the high six-figures, the greatest share contributed by the company and the Hughes family, with a lesser amount (somewhat more than the figure it had set aside for legal expenses) kicked in by the insurance company. Just weeks after the settlement, Harlan sold Prosperity Oil Inc. and all its wells to one of the larger oil producers in the Appalachian Basin. Though the price was not disclosed, rumors circulated in the oil patch that Harlan Hughes and his family suffered a financial hosing in the deal.

William Jeffries, Ginny Weed's attorney, broke with legal tradition and refused to accept as compensation the entire one-third of the settlement stipulated in his engagement contract. He instead carefully itemized his hours from the beginning of the case and charged Ginny an hourly rate that was in the mid-range for legal work in the region, an amount totaling slightly less than ten percent of the settlement. Certain professional colleagues, aghast by this worrisome precedent, incredulously asked him why he didn't take all the money owed to him under the contract.

"It just didn't seem the right thing to do," replied Jeffries unapologetically. "I would have felt ashamed profiting excessively from that poor family's misfortune, particularly when I see them at church each Sunday."

□ □ □ CASE #2—WALTER SCHULMANN:
"HE HAS TEN FINGERS AND SURELY WON'T MISS A FEW."

Walter Schulmann loved Lance Greenwald like a brother, which made their falling out (and subsequent lawsuit) all the more painful to bear. Lance Greenwald had worked for Walter for almost seven years, during which time Walter's company, Heavenly Hardwood Inc., had grown from a small woodworking shop specializing in church pews to a major manufacturer of upscale garden furniture. Walter never viewed Lance as an employee; he was his esteemed colleague and trusted friend, his cornerstone, his inspiration, and, as the company's master woodworker, his indispensable right-hand man. In hindsight, it was perversely ironic that Lance lost most of his right hand in such a gruesome industrial accident.

The big break for the company occurred two years before, when a national chain of home improvement stores began carrying several of its products. The big seller, designed by Lance, was a simple but elegant park bench, combining maple and cherry hardwoods in a striking geometric pattern. The benches sold briskly and Heavenly Hardwood Inc. had a difficult time filling the backlogged orders. Other retailers queried the company about its product line, but Walter didn't even have time to respond. Every machine and every employee worked overtime making furniture.

As usual, Lance came up with a brilliant new plan, one that would simultaneously boost production and increase profit margins. Instead of buying finished hardwood lumber, as they'd been doing, Lance proposed buying low-cost, rough-cut boards from a down-state saw-mill and finishing the lumber themselves. They could then purchase more cross-cut and ripping saws, more joiners, and hire several more workers to operate them and assemble product, essentially funding company growth through material savings. It was an interesting idea, but Walter, ever practical and cautious, questioned whether it would work. He knew that finishing lumber would require an oversized planer that would cost a bundle, offsetting any savings from buying unfinished lumber.

Lance Greenwald's eyes grew bright with excitement. Having thought through this economic obstacle, Lance revealed the second part of his plan. "I found a planer. It's a behemoth, a real monster, probably eighty, ninety years old. It's been in storage and hasn't been used in about a half-century. I know I can update it to serve our needs. I found it in Amish country the last time I went looking for additional hardwood suppliers."

The planer he'd found, a precision tool for its day, weighed almost a thousand pounds and had a massive steel bed and oversized blades that were as sound as the day it was made. At one time, it had been driven by a huge belt and flywheel, undoubtedly one of many wood-working machines lined up and powered by a single, steam-driven engine. The broad planer had clearly been made when old-growth timber was still plentiful, yielding wide boards seldom seen today. The flywheel had been removed, probably long ago, though a short rotating shaft that once connected to it still remained, extending beyond the table, a jagged reminder of a bygone industrial era. Lance had worked out a fantastic deal with the planer's owner, whose deceased father had once operated a small lumber mill. For decades, the planer stood untouched in a large shed, covered by a canvas tarp encrusted with dust and pigeon droppings.

Confident in Lance's assessment, Walter agreed to buy the planer sight unseen, and the two men immediately went to close the deal and arrange for its transfer. The owner seemed just another country yokel until he pulled out a legal document and asked Walter to sign it as a condition of sale. The document read:

> Purchaser, Heavenly Hardwood, Inc., hereby accepts the planer in "as is" condition, with no warranties or performance representations whatsoever by Seller regarding said machine. Heavenly Hardwoods, Inc. further acknowledges and accepts that said planer is not OSHA compliant and, in its current condition, is extremely hazardous to operate. Heavenly Hardwoods Inc. agrees to indemnify and hold harmless the Seller from all claims, suits, judgments. . .

Walter handed the document to Lance, more of a dismissive gesture than actually seeking his comment. Despite being an accomplished business owner, Walter had little experience in legal matters; he always felt uncomfortable when asked to sign legal documents, particularly ones popped on him unexpectedly. What at first seemed an uncomplicated, secondhand purchase had suddenly turned into an anxiety-provoking deal with apparent legal implications. Walter reflexively made light of the owner's request and cracked a stupid joke, a regrettable comment that will probably bother him for the rest of his life.

"Sure I'll sign," he said with a shrug and a laugh. "Lance here is the one who'll be operating the planer and taking the risk. Why, he's so talented, he could feed lumber with his elbows, or his tongue even, if it ever ate his hands."

The owner frowned, obviously put off by Walter's comment. "My dad lost two fingers to that cursed machine," he said quietly.

Mortified, Walter muttered a quick apology and said nothing else, eager to complete the deal and end the embarrassing situation. He quickly signed the acknowledgment and indemnification agreement, handed the man a check, and arranged to retrieve the planer at the end of the following week.

"Why delay the delivery?" asked Lance, eager to work on the machine and put it into production.

"I wanted to wait until after OSHA's follow-up inspection next Tuesday," answered Walter. "We've had enough citations already. We don't need any more. Besides, I want you to get that behemoth up and going without some know-nothing OSHA inspector telling you what you can and cannot do with it."

OSHA had been an irritant for the company ever since an unscheduled inspection the previous year. Heavenly Hardwood Inc. had never had a serious accident or injury in its entire eight years in business, nothing more than a few minor cuts and bruises, but the nitpicking inspectors, the "OSHA Gestapo" as he called them, had cited the company for about a half-dozen violations, including inadequate eye protection and excessive airborne wood dust in the shop. Walter got steamed just hearing the word "OSHA." In his mind, his company deserved a medal, not another bloody citation, which surely would come if the inspector saw the behemoth planer in its present condition.

After the planer had been moved to the shop, Lance spent two days installing a huge new electric motor, adjusting and cleaning the moving parts, and carefully balancing and leveling the machine. Walter and about a dozen others gathered around to watch Lance fire it up for the first time. Lance carefully fed a wide slab of knotty maple through it and the whirling blade took off a full quarter-inch as if it were butter, the planer screaming like a banshee for the full twenty seconds it took to complete the process. Even Lance looked a little shaken by the machine's furious power.

"I don't want anyone touching this machine except Lance," said Walter after the planer powered down. "It is extremely dangerous without machine guarding. Until we figure out the needed safety modifications, I want everyone to stay clear."

Lance continued making minor adjustments and just before lunch started feeding a variety of hardwoods through the planer to test it further. The planer's loud, high-pitched screeching drowned out the other woodworking machines and put everyone on edge. Despite the noise, however, nearly everyone heard Lance's horrific scream as the planer whittled away four fingers and much of his palm, leaving only his thumb dangling oddly from his grotesquely mutilated right hand. Walter and everyone else in the shop came running. Lance stood beside the planer holding his mangled hand, a look of utter disbelief on his face. Incongruously, he was bare-chested. The remnants of his shirt flapped madly in the whirling shaft extending beyond the planer's table. Bits of flesh and bone, some as perfectly sliced as bologna from the deli, dotted the crimson wood-shavings beside the machine.

Cradling his hand, Lance never said a word as he waited for the ambulance to arrive, his face ashen and eyes glazed. Walter, meanwhile, bounced around completely agitated, overwhelmed with emotion and dismay. He tried unsuccessfully to comfort Lance, breathlessly saying again and again as if a broken record, "You're going to be OK, you're going to be OK." Walter finally shut up when Lance slowly looked up at him hatefully, silently admonishing him, correcting his misconception with a venomous stare.

Investigation and Aftermath

Tipped off by an anonymous phone call, OSHA dispatched two compliance officers the next day to investigate the accident. Needless to say, Heavenly Hardwood Inc. was cited for multiple "willful" and "serious" violations of the machine guarding and other safety standards and fined $46,254. Based on the physical evidence coupled with Lance's recollections, the OSHA investigators determined that Lance's un-tucked shirt had wound around the unprotected, rotating shaft of the planer, flinging him into the blade and ripping his shirt from his back in the blink of an eye.

Lance had a miserable time recovering, his convalescence com-plicated by an intractable infection and allergic reactions to his wide range of pain medications. He relied mostly on Tylenol rather than endure the debilitating nausea brought on by the more powerful drugs. Walter visited him at the hospital after the accident, exhibiting a feigned upbeat attitude that Lance found so grating he asked him to leave and stay away until he felt better.

During his second night at the hospital, nearly demented from pain-induced insomnia, Lance grew increasingly fearful and resentful over what had happened to him. All his professional talents required the use of his two hands, and without one he questioned his ability to function in the future. He had lost his most important appendage— and for what? For a measly paycheck? For the enrichment of Walter Schulmann? As the excruciating hours ticked by slowly, Lance boiled with rage and rancor.

Meanwhile, Walter also spent sleepless nights worrying about Lance and obsessing about the accident. Rocked to his very soul, Wal-ter felt horrified by what had happened. He regarded Lance so highly, had so trusted Lance's judgment and expertise, that he could hardly believe his friend had been so gravely injured. Walter recognized he owed much of the company's success to Lance. He resolved to take care of Lance financially, help him recover, and make him an equity partner in the business. After all, Walter depended more on Lance's leadership and creativity than on his hands.

After further medical evaluation, the doctors amputated Lance's thumb and the remnants of his hand, deciding he'd be better off with a full-hand prosthesis. While hospitalized, Lance refused to see visitors and answer phone calls. Consequently, Walter never had the oppor-tunity to reassure his friend. When he finally did see Lance after his discharge from the hospital, his mood was so unfriendly that Walter had second thoughts about making Lance his partner, instinctively adopting a "wait and see" attitude.

After three months of rehabilitation, Walter and Lance's coworkers warmly welcomed Lance back to work, with everyone sincerely pleased to see him. Sadly, Lance had been profoundly altered by the accident. Previously confident and positive, he was now pessimistic and acerbic, emotionally struggling with his disability and new limitations. Despite Walter's sincere efforts to accommodate Lance and find him meaningful assignments, Lance responded with frustration and hostility. "Make-work for the cripple," he'd often mutter under his breath.

Lance's sour disposition cast a shadow over the entire company, and coworkers began to avoid him, which only made things worse. For a few months, Walter patiently tolerated his disagreeable behavior, hoping that time would heal all. It didn't. The blowup occurred when Lance savagely demolished a new bench he'd been designing, his anger ignited when a wooden slat kept slipping from his prosthetic hand. Drawn to the disturbance, Walter likewise lost his temper and instructed Lance to leave the premises at once. He also told Lance not to return unless he changed his contemptible attitude. Lance never did.

Lance retained an attorney and filed an intentional-tort suit against Heavenly Hardwood Inc. for the loss of his hand and sought $1 million in damages for his pain and suffering. With the help of a private investigator, Lance's attorney methodically built a strong case, jump-started by OSHA's damning and well-documented investigative report. OSHA had concluded that Lance's injury had been "substantially certain" to have occurred given the machine's multiple safety shortcomings. The investigator obtained a sworn affidavit from the former owner of the planer, who recounted Walter's comments regarding Lance's using "his elbows" to push lumber through the planer if it ever "ate his hands." The former owner's statement detailed his efforts to warn Walter that the planer was "an extreme hazard," recounting how his father had been seriously injured using the same machine, a fact that had been disclosed to Walter. A copy of the agreement signed by Walter at the time of purchase was stapled to the affidavit as supporting evidence.

The investigator also obtained statements from several coworkers who confirmed Walter's comments that the planer was an "extreme" hazard without the necessary machine guarding required by law. Two worker statements recounted Walter's contempt for OSHA and its safety standards, evidenced by his referring to OSHA inspectors as the "OSHA Gestapo." Lance's suit was further strengthened by Walter's purposely delaying delivery of the planer to avoid detection by OSHA inspectors, a fact that Walter grudgingly confirmed later during deposition.

With so much strong evidence, Lance's attorney easily overcame the company's efforts to have the suit thrown out under the "exclusive remedy" argument and the case was scheduled for trial. During this time, Walter raved and ranted about the unfairness of the lawsuit. "How could I have 'intentionally' injured Lance," he fumed. "It was Lance's idea to buy that damned planer in the first place! If anyone intentionally hurt Lance, it was Lance who hurt himself."

Walter's attorney persuaded Walter to settle after the deposition of the planer's prior owner. His moving testimony painted Walter as a despicably insensitive person, unconcerned about the inherent dangers of the machine, joking about its maiming Lance. The prior owner tearfully recounted how his father had lost fingers in the planer and how he'd "never been the same" afterwards. "I know just how this poor man feels," he said, referring to Lance in a quavering voice. Walter's attorney said he'd never heard more compelling (and damaging) testimony from a witness.

The lawsuit was eventually settled for an undisclosed sum, reportedly in the mid-six-figures, half paid by the company and half by its insurance. Walter had to wrangle with his insurance company to ensure its participation in the settlement. Neither Lance nor Walter have recovered from the experience. Lance remains embittered, having lost his sense of confidence and self-worth in addition to his hand. Walter lost his best friend, a lot of money, and the innocent satisfactions of a collegial working environment. The company's business has fallen off considerably, with fewer new products to replace those that have faded from consumer favor. The remaining employees have also suffered, shaken by the psychic and physical mutilation of a respected colleague, dispirited by the divisive legal controversy, and distrustful of a future where bad things truly do happen to good people.

Putting production before safety is probably the worst operational mistake a business can make. Businesses that do so may avoid the consequences for a while, but a day of reckoning will surely come. Wise managers understand that it is nearly impossible to save money by scrimping on employee health and safety. On the flip side, spending money on health and safety saves money in the long run, with fewer work days lost to illness and injury, markedly lower insurance costs, better employee loyalty and morale, and (most importantly) the avoidance of costly lawsuits and injury claims that can destabilize a business.

Many employers ascribe to the safety credo of the self-deceived, sharing the delusion that because serious accidents haven't happened they won't happen. Government statistics suggest the opposite. According to the U.S. Department of Labor, more than 10,000 workers die and 6,200,000 are injured each year in work-related accidents in the United States. Furthermore, an estimated 100,000 workers die yearly from illnesses arising from toxic chemical exposure, often the consequence of unsafe workplace practices from decades earlier. Interestingly, midsized companies with 50 to 500 employees have significantly higher rates of injury and illness than smaller and larger companies.

To their subsequent regret, many employers fail to take health and safety seriously until a serious accident compels a change in attitude and practice—a wake-up call that can become a goodnight call in some instances. As these cases demonstrate, employers with an indifferent attitude toward safety may find themselves besieged by legal and financial woes when an employee gets killed or seriously hurt. Prudent employers should ponder what could result from their inattentiveness.

In the early decades of the twentieth century, every state in the union adopted workers' compensation laws to assure the fast and efficient delivery of disability and medical benefits to injured workers, speeding their return to gainful employment at a reasonable cost to employers. The workers' compensation system required the renunciation of common-law rights and defenses by both employers and employees, allowing both to avoid the uncertainties of litigation. In return for accepting liability for all workplace injuries and illnesses regardless of fault and, in addition, surrendering traditional legal defenses, an employer could thereafter treat workers' compensation benefits as a routine business expense that could be budgeted without worry about adverse court judgments.

Similarly, by relinquishing traditional tort remedies for a system of compensation without contest, employees were spared the cost, delay, and uncertainty of asserting a legal claim. By design, workers' compensation statutes limit an employee's ability to recover medical treatment and wage-loss benefits resulting from a work-related illness or accident. These defined benefits were intended to be a worker's sole remedy for occupational illnesses and injuries. Under the "exclusive remedy" doctrine, employers are supposed to be immune from worker lawsuits based on common-law theories of personal injury.

With legal inventiveness, plaintiff lawyers have challenged the exclusive remedy doctrine in thousands of lawsuits on behalf of injured workers, petitioning courts nationwide to find exceptions to the doctrine and award damages under common-law tort rules. Most states now recognize at least some exceptions to exclusivity, allowing claimants to bring legal action directly against their employers. In several key decisions, the supreme court of my home state, Ohio, has strongly affirmed that promoting workplace safety is an overriding public policy goal and correspondingly has refused to let employers hide behind the limited liability of worker's compensation while committing intentional acts.

Where Ohio's Supreme Court broke new ground, with other state courts duly taking notice, is in the interpretation of intentional conduct. In short, the court posed a special definition for "intentional tort" in the employment context, going beyond the traditional meaning for intentional torts—acts deliberately committed with the desire to injure another—to now include employer's actions (or inactions) from which an employee's injury or illness was "substantially certain" to occur. While few employers intentionally try to hurt their employees, some employers engage in conduct that is so dangerous that an intent to injure can be inferred.

Under this special definition, an injured worker need only prove that the employer 1) knew the condition at issue was dangerous yet required the employee to work under that dangerous condition, and 2) knew that harm to the employee was substantially certain to occur. Of course, determining if an illness or injury was substantially certain to occur requires, in most cases, a jury to decide. Once in the courtroom, even remote possibilities can turn into substantial certainties in the eyes of jurors, particularly in those cases with the most emotional wallop—those combining horrific injury or death with the wanton recklessness or gross negligence by the employer. The lawsuits arising from Benny Weed's death and Lance Greenwald's injury had this combination, and both defendant companies were well advised to settle before trial. In such cases, juries may be more concerned with dispensing justice than compensating for actual losses, applying the "make 'em pay" approach when computing awards. Furthermore, juries decide common-law intentional tort claims on the basis of a "preponderance of evidence" versus the more rigorous "clear and convincing" standard of proof, making it relatively easy to side with sympathetic plaintiffs.

Employers must understand that certain actions (or inactions) can later be used by plaintiff attorneys to bolster an intentional tort case. By delaying delivery of the planer, Walter Schulmann purposely evaded an OSHA safety inspection, knowing the planer did not comply with OSHA's machine guarding standards. He also ignored the seller's warnings regarding the machine's inherently hazardous condition. Various factors—such as keeping equipment in a defective condition, ignoring reports of potential hazards, and concealing or intentionally misstating dangers—can all support a jury's verdict that an employer engaged in conduct substantially certain to cause employee injuries.

The legal distinction between specific intent to injure (intentional tort) and endangering the health of workers (negligence) often becomes blurred in lawsuits involving toxic chemicals. All employers have a legal duty to keep the workplace free from recognized hazards that cause, or are likely to cause, death or serious injury to employees. Under the "Hazard Communication Standard" (29 CFR 1910.1200), employers have a legal obligation to develop a written hazard communication program to identify hazardous chemicals in the workplace and to develop a plan for informing employees of those hazards. Harlan Hughes could not claim ignorance in regard to the dangers of toluene or his duty to inform his pumpers. Harlan had been provided detailed safety information by the chemical distributor, acknowledged in writing by Harlan, yet he made no effort to comply with the recommended safe-handling guidelines or to inform his pumpers about toluene's perils.

Harlan cooked his own goose by intentionally concealing the toluene from both local and federal authorities, neglecting to post the appropriate hazard warnings, and failing to make available the "material safety data sheets" as required by law to the pumpers using the chemical. Courts and jurors are more inclined to find accidents as having been "substantially certain" to occur when employers engage in deceit and misrepresentation in addition to irresponsible behavior. When an employer like Harlan withholds from employees essential information regarding a known hazard that poses a serious threat of injury, thereby impeding the employees from exercising their own informed judgment whether to perform the assigned task, the employer will likely be found to have acted with the knowledge that harm was substantially certain to occur.

In addition to his deliberate failure to observe even basic safety laws, Harlan dug himself further into a legal hole by economically coercing his employees, telling them that the company's economic viability and their future employment required their handling toluene. In truth, Harlan could count himself lucky to avoid a criminal indictment and negotiate a reasonable settlement before trial. A jury might well have meted out more serious financial punishment given the facts of the case.

Harlan and Walter both made the foolish yet not uncommon mistake of treating a hazardous condition and employee safety as a laughing matter. Employers must always remember that subject dictates tone when communicating with employees. In other words, there is nothing funny whatsoever about workplace hazards and employee accidents. Joking about these and other serious issues weakens employee morale and drives a wedge between employer and employees. Nothing undermines worker loyalty more than the perception that management cares more about profits than worker health and safety. Serious accidents harden employee misgivings and produce a strained, adversarial atmosphere that can poison a workplace.

Offhand comments said in jest can later become compelling evidence of wanton disregard for employee safety. Employers should always remember that whatever they say can and will be used against them in a court of law. In almost every intentional tort lawsuit, there is a point where wanton negligence or reckless behavior crosses the line such that the ensuing accident could be perceived as a substantial certainty. Harlan's and Walter's thoughtless jokes may have tipped the legal scales in each case. Perhaps events would have been wholly different had both responded with sincere and attentive concern—not an inconsiderate joke—when the issue of safety was raised.

But what about the culpability of the victims? Were not Benny and Lance guilty of contributory negligence? After all, Benny likely inhaled the toluene vapor purposely to get high. Lance Greenwald found the planer and knew all about its safety shortcomings, yet took it upon himself to modify the machine and test it without asking for expert assistance. Shouldn't the two victims have been held somewhat accountable, thereby sparing their employers at least some of the liability? Such thinking may seem reasonable but almost never holds up in the courtroom. "Blame the victim" frequently backfires as a defense strategy. Under the law, employers are held to a higher standard of care than employees, much like the parent-child relationship. The employer has the legal duty to provide a safe working environment—not the employee.

In hindsight, Walter abdicated his responsibility as an employer by not questioning Lance's judgment concerning the purchase and modification of a defective machine. Such mistakes happen every day in workplaces around America, occasionally resulting in dreadful accidents. Highly confident and capable people like Lance generally kindle excessive trust in their ideas and leadership. Colleagues and coworkers will often follow them right off a cliff. Bold, creative thinking must be always tempered with cautious, methodical implementation. After receiving an explicit warning of the planer's hazardous condition, Walter should have had it professionally evaluated and modified under a mechanical engineer's supervision, adding machine safety guards as required by OSHA standards. With such an approach, there would have been nothing to fear from OSHA's scheduled inspection. In fact, the OSHA inspector might have helped immensely. Most experienced safety professionals would have instantly identified the danger of the unguarded, rotating shaft extending beyond the planer's table. The extension no longer served any function and could have been (and should have been) removed. In hindsight, cutting off the shaft extension would have been considerably less costly for Heavenly Hardwoods Inc. than Lance's losing his hand.

Companies are especially vulnerable to serious workplace accidents during times of declining revenues and rapid growth. Financial pressures can lead to cost- and corner-cutting with obvious safety implications, and backlog pressures can hurry changes in manufacturing processes where safety issues take a backseat to boosting production. Cost and production concerns almost always play a role in workplace safety lapses. Harlan tried to save a nickel but lost a fortune by taking on the well-treatments while oblivious to the hazards. Walter carelessly went along with a hurried action plan, slighting the safety risks in favor of increased output. "We can't afford it" is, of course, the most common excuse for neglecting safety, often followed by, "We'll do it when we have the money," added as if to mitigate guilt. The cost of a dead employee, however, dwarfs any potential savings in subcontractor fees.

Employers have both a moral and a legal duty to protect their employees from workplace hazards. Those employers who recognize and act on that duty need not fear employee lawsuits for workplace illnesses and accidents. On the other hand, self-centered and avaricious employers who care little about their workers have much to fear when accidents inevitably occur. The specter of costly lawsuits and judgments should prod any employers into implementing sensible compliance and safety programs. Though heartfelt concern for others is always the better motivator, the legal whip of liability should serve as a substitute for those who don't feel the sting of conscience.

To avoid liability for workplace accidents and illnesses, *all* employers should become obsessive about workplace safety. First and foremost, employers must research all applicable standards, laws, and regulations to determine which apply to them and which do not. Safety issues vary considerably from business to business. A hospital, for example, must heed numerous regulations concerning the hazards of blood-borne pathogens, while a trucking company must follow scores of regulations on securing loads and distributing cargo weight. After identifying all applicable safety laws and regulations, employers must systematically implement and document a compliance program to ensure they are scrupulously followed.

All prudent and responsible employers should establish and maintain a safety program that provides systematic policies, procedures, and practices designed to identify and protect employees from occupational safety and health hazards. For a program to be effective, management must regard worker safety and health as a fundamental value of the organization and demonstrate its commitment to safety and health protection with as much energy as to other organizational purposes. Employee involvement is essential for any such program's success. Employees must feel empowered and have a clear, defined role in protecting themselves and their coworkers.

Employers should carefully create and preserve written documentation confirming their sincere efforts to comply with health and safety laws. Since 1990, a number of states have passed laws requiring employers to adopt written safety and health programs. Many other states are considering similar legislation. Various OSHA standards—such as the Hazard Communication Standard—require written evidence of compliance. When enforcing standards that specifically require written programs, OSHA inspectors operate under the premise that, "If it isn't written, you don't have one." A company can earnestly preach about the safe handling of a toxic chemical, but would still be cited and fined by OSHA if its hazard communication program isn't written down.

Correct documentation can help prevent employee lawsuits, or provide a strong defense if one is ever filed. Had Harlan Hughes simply told his pumpers to be careful and distributed the manufacturer's "material safety data sheets" describing toluene's toxicity and volatility, Harlan might well have prevailed in his motion for summary judgment, or even at trial. His safety efforts would still have been woefully inadequate, but he would have had irrefutable documentary evidence of his efforts to warn his pumpers about toluene's dangers.

In many intentional tort lawsuits, the employee takes the position that the employer caused the accident by failing to provide proper training. No sane worker would purposely hurt himself, but given the facts of some accidents, you sometimes have to wonder. After an employee loses a hand in a hydraulic press, he's more likely to say, "My supervisor didn't tell me not to" than "I'm such an idiot for putting my hand in there." Some workers can be incomprehensibly careless. Employers have a legal duty, through proper supervision and training, to keep such dunderheads from hurting themselves.

There are more than 200 OSHA standards that include training or special qualifications for certain job assignments. Employer should know which ones apply to their businesses and abide by the training requirements. Though only a few OSHA standards specifically require written documentation of safety training, prudent employers should document every training program, creating a detailed record that includes the names of the employees present, the date, the name of the trainer and the trainer's qualifications, and a summary of information covered. It would be very difficult for an employee to prevail in a lawsuit on the basis of no training when his signature appears on a training attendance sheet.

In order to be legally compliant, however, safety training must be proper, conveying practical and accurate information consistent with the safety standards for the particular business or industry. In other words, an employer must make sure that the content of the training and the qualifications of the trainer are reasonable and prudent based on workplace circumstances. Employers often make the mistake of relying on a single individual with few qualifications to manage their safety and training programs. In many cases, the safety manager's only qualification is completion of a forty-hour OSHA "Train the Trainer" course, which really doesn't mean much at all. Even an imbecile can become an "authorized OSHA trainer" simply by sitting in class for a week. At the conclusion of the course, attendees are not required to demonstrate that they learned anything by having to pass an examination. When I completed the OSHA "Train the Trainer" course many years ago, I received the same embossed certificate as one classmate who literally slept the week away in the seat behind me. I wonder how capable and effective a safety trainer that narcoleptic has been for his employer? How skilled has he been at identifying and eliminating workplace hazards? I shudder to think.

Unfortunately, ineptitude at hazard recognition pervades many if not most workplaces. Myopic employers are not alone. Even OSHA inspectors have been known to overlook serious violations and imminent dangers during comprehensive workplace assessments, though dutifully issuing citations for *de minimus* conditions. To focus their attention and trigger action, employers must adopt a paranoid attitude and expect that a serious workplace accident or illness is just waiting to happen, a time bomb that must be found and disarmed before it goes off. Every nook and cranny of the business should be inspected looking for it.

Few employers, however, have the in-house expertise to conduct a systematic safety audit of all facilities and business operations. For this reason, enlisting an outside expert to assist in safety audits accomplishes a number of important objectives. For one, a trained safety professional should be able to identify most workplace hazards and provide clear advice on how to eliminate them. Additionally, after engaging a professional and implementing safety recommendations, an employer can relax somewhat, knowing any subsequent accidents will almost surely fail to meet the legal criteria for an intentional tort, thereby ensuring that the financial and legal exposures will be limited to claims through the workers' compensation system. Even if the safety professional overlooks an imminent danger and an accident occurs as a consequence, an employer might well have a claim against the professional, who surely carries "errors and omissions" insurance, preferably with very high limits. In addition to getting good analysis and advice, engaging a qualified safety expert buys another layer of insurance coverage along with documentation that will be useful as a defense against intentional tort lawsuits.

Outside expertise need not be costly. Every state in the country offers free safety consultations to employers, funded largely by money from OSHA. In Ohio, the Department of Commerce's Division of Labor and Worker Safety administers our state program. State safety experts, upon written request from an employer, will conduct comprehensive or problem-specific safety reviews. With the exception of imminent life-threatening violations, these inspectors will not report adverse findings to OSHA, nor will they issue citations. Instead, they will provide employers with an appraisal of all identifiable workplace hazards and critique operational practices. In addition, they will evaluate the existing safety and health program or help establish a new one. They will also provide free training and assistance with implementing recommendations. By participating in a state-sponsored consultation program, employers can demonstrate a written record of good-faith efforts to comply with safety laws and regulations, thereby attaining further protection from intentional tort lawsuits.

Employers should never forget that their mission is to ensure worker safety by enforcing compliance with safety standards and regulations, a noble task that sometimes requires being petty. Whenever employers complain about OSHA, I ask them to identify just one standard they believe ridiculous or unfair. They never can. Employers should always remember that those who comply have little to fear from OSHA or, for that matter, from many of the legal, medical, workers' compensation, and other intangible costs of accidents.

Employers often have difficulty grasping the full value of safety programs. After all, how do you calculate the savings from events that thankfully never occur? The lessons learned from workplace accidents and injuries are often expensive ones, paid in blood and pain in addition to dollars. Better and less costly lessons come from effective safeguarding, safety training, hazard analysis and communication, and sincere self-auditing.

As an investigator, I am haunted by many past cases where decent people got badly injured or killed on the job, destroying their own lives and those of others. The effects of serious workplace accidents linger long after the blood has been mopped. Torn bodies and psyches may never completely heal. Witnesses are often among the walking wounded, forever traumatized by the ghastly images seared into their memories. I sometimes wonder about people like Lance Greenwald,

Walter Schulmann, Harlan Hughes, and Benny Weed and how their lives might have turned out differently. Few things in life create regret quite like preventable accidents and illnesses. They gnaw at our happiness and peace of mind, sometimes for lifetimes, sometimes even for generations.

▫ ▫ ▫ **CAUTIONARY TIPS:**

- Just because a serious accident hasn't happened doesn't mean it won't happen
- Spending money on safety is more sensible than spending money on lawsuits, disability payments, and higher insurance premiums.

CHAPTER 6

Asset Misappropriation in the Workplace

□ □ □ **CASE #1—COURTNEY KOSSUTH:**
"HE'D NEVER DO THAT—WHY, HE'S LIKE ONE OF OUR FAMILY"

Courtney Kossuth had the daunting and, in hindsight, unenviable task of replacing her father, Tivadar Kossuth, as CEO of Fox Run Ltd., a successful holding company that designed, built, and managed commercial real estate projects throughout the state. Now retired and in declining health in Florida, Tivadar had been a legendary developer in his day, a man who'd started with almost nothing and ended with almost everything. The only son of Eastern European immigrants, hard-driving Tivadar made his fortune by first building tract houses and later strip malls in outlying areas where cows had been grazing just a few years before. The firm now had more than 100 full-time employees—property managers and custodians, designers and draftsmen, construction workers and tradesmen, project managers and bookkeepers—a bustling array of good people who kept the great enterprise going. Of the many employees, none was considered more respected or more indispensable than Patrick O'Malley, the chief financial officer, who'd been with the company almost from the beginning. Courtney and her siblings had grown up referring to him affectionately as "Uncle Patrick," though he was not a blood relation.

Everyone connected with the company knew that Patrick O'Malley actually ran the business, and that Courtney owed her lofty position to good old-fashioned nepotism. Fox Run Ltd. had always been and would always remain a family-owned company. After Tivadar retired abruptly with heart problems, Patrick O'Malley ran the business for almost a year until the appointment of Courtney, the youngest of the four siblings and the only responsible child among an otherwise underachieving lot. Like so many children of the ultra-successful, the Kossuth children (Courtney excluded) never amounted to much of anything. The oldest daughter had been working on her Ph.D. in

Romantic literature for sixteen years, the process prolonged by several failed marriages. The two boys were equally ineffectual: the older son lived a bohemian life in NYC making odd sculptures only his ingratiating friends would ever consider buying, while the younger son approached his troubled psyche as his full-time job, embracing every new therapy (including intestinal irrigation) in an effort to overcome his persistent and paralyzing ennui. Other than the size of the dividend checks sent them each month, Courtney's siblings had no interest whatsoever in Fox Run Ltd., which was probably a good thing.

In hindsight, Courtney sensed there would be problems her very first day as CEO. Admittedly unqualified to run the business, she had wanted to start at a lower position, but her domineering father wanted a Kossuth at the helm, mentored by Uncle Pat, who knew the business inside and out. Only thirty years old and a business neophyte, Courtney had worked (quite successfully) as a fund-raiser for the local symphony orchestra while also writing a lively local arts column for a suburban newspaper. To address her limited experience before joining the company, Courtney completed an executive MBA program at the local community college, a weekend program completed mostly by middle managers hoping to jump-start their stalled careers. Rather than boosting her confidence, however, the program mostly reminded Courtney of how little she knew about business and the many challenges involved in managing a multimillion dollar enterprise.

As Courtney's designated mentor, Patrick O'Malley was not especially helpful as she tried to learn the business as its new CEO. He was like the swimming instructor who throws the beginner into the deep end and advises her not to drown. Knowing both she and the company depended on "Uncle Patrick," Courtney acknowledged his leadership role on her first day, deferentially telling him that he, not she, should have been named CEO by her father. Courtney remembered how Patrick had said nothing and just smiled at her, a cool smile without friendliness, silently communicating he believed the same. She instantly felt uncomfortable. Her intuition told her that Patrick would be a problem, but like so many other "good girls," Courtney resolved to win him over with kindness, courtesy, and hard work.

Thirty years before, Tivadar Kossuth had hired Patrick O'Malley as an entry-level bookkeeper. The young man had been eager to rise above his modest, working-class background. At the start, he worked days and attended community college at night, eventually earning an accounting degree. Impressed by his ambition and work ethic, Tivadar promoted Patrick to increasingly responsible positions, including the management of several valuable properties, and eventually made him the company's CFO in charge of all financial planning and oversight. When Courtney joined the company as CEO, Patrick was earning about $160,000 per year, a substantial but not an enriching salary considering he had six children, including three in college and one with special needs.

On her first day, Patrick told Courtney that as CEO, her dad spent his time mostly outside the office making things happen. "I did the paperwork and he did the deals," Patrick had said. He saw that as her job now and suggested she start by visiting the company properties, saying Courtney should see what they'd accomplished in the past in order to give her ideas for the future. He also suggested she contact several established developers who might be interested in joint ventures. Though civil and seemingly respectful, Patrick insinuated she was too inexperienced to initiate and manage development projects on her own.

Courtney compliantly followed Pat's advice. In truth, familiarizing herself with the company's property portfolio seemed a reasonable way to begin, though Courtney wondered if Patrick just wanted to be rid of her, a suspicion reinforced by his indifferent and unhelpful background briefings before she set out. Over the ensuing weeks, she visited all sixteen properties owned by the company, including apartment complexes, retail malls, and office buildings. At first, she asked few questions, passively touring the properties as if simply admiring their aesthetics. Courtney soon became more discerning, however, and grew more comfortable questioning the on-site property managers about maintenance expenses, capital requirements, occupancy rates, and other operational issues. In the back of her mind, she wanted to win Pat's respect and approval by learning the business without unduly burdening him in the process.

On her own initiative, Courtney developed a list of questions to help her assess the operations and profitability of each property. The firm's profits came mostly from its real estate holdings, not from construction revenues, and Courtney thought it best to understand the cash flows. She was stymied, however, because none of the property managers could answer all her questions regarding income and expenses, often responding by saying, "You'll have to ask Patrick for that information." Courtney learned that many financial matters were handled by Patrick O'Malley at corporate headquarters.

In fact, none of the site managers could precisely figure the profitability of the individual properties, largely because headquarters collected tenant payments and paid many of the larger operating expenses, such as utility bills and contractor fees. For the most part, the property managers mostly handled petty purchases for such things as light bulbs and cleaning supplies, and even these items were often supplied by the company, presumably saving money by purchasing in bulk. Site managers generally would only learn if a tenant fell behind in the rent if called by Pat, who'd periodically direct them to pound on the tenant's door and demand payment, even if it was only a week or two late. Believing collection the handmaid of profitability, Patrick O'Malley had always pressed for every dollar owed the company.

Between property tours, Courtney met with Patrick to request the financial data she'd been unable to obtain directly from the site managers. Though outwardly agreeable, she could sense Pat's vexation as he jotted down her areas of interest, always noncommittal as to when she might receive it. To Courtney's frustration, the data Patrick would eventually provide was neither complete nor precisely in the format requested. After six weeks and still feeling almost as confused as on her first day, Courtney asked Patrick in exasperation why he was making things difficult for her. Certainly he tracked the financial performance of each property, and she simply couldn't understand why he wouldn't share this information with her.

For the first time, Patrick openly expressed hostility. Through slightly clenched teeth, he said he hadn't the time to answer all her questions and resented her questioning his competence. He ranted for some minutes about how the company's finances were complicated, how the headquarters' overhead and certain expenses had to be allocated to all the firm's holdings. Patrick disclosed that some maintenance contracts, such as garbage collection and snow removal, encompassed multiple properties. He then reminded Courtney that her job was to generate new business, not to question him on how he did his. Her monthly dividend checks, he snidely pointed out, should be ample evidence of the solid profitability of Fox Run Ltd.

Though shocked by his words, Courtney remained calm and denied questioning his competence, insisting she was only trying to understand the business, nothing more. She reminded him that he had recommended she analyze past successes before initiating any new investments. Courtney then politely asked Patrick to share his financial analysis, in whatever format that suited him, for at least one representative property. Courtney suggested The Pinnacle, a commercial property she planned to visit several days later. Patrick muttered something under his breath but agreed to provide her something, though he couldn't promise she'd have it before her visit.

Despite its exalted name, The Pinnacle was a tired and unassuming office building situated among even lesser buildings in an older section of town. Stephan Froelich, a wiry old-timer who'd been with the firm for decades, managed the building. What Stephan told Courtney during her visit would begin Patrick O'Malley's downfall.

A likable and uncomplicated man, Stephan got right into it when Courtney asked about the building and its management issues. He expressed incredulity that Patrick O'Malley could be so concerned about saving money on some things while wasting money on others. As an example, Stephan mentioned snow removal. Previously, he had shoveled the walkways himself and his cousin had plowed the parking lot, charging just twenty bucks per plow. His cousin got paid only if it snowed, which wasn't often, considering recent winters had been so mild. For some incomprehensible reason, last winter Patrick had engaged a firm under a seasonal contract, paying top dollar whether it snowed or not. Shaking his head, Stephan observed that Courtney's dad would never have allowed such an inexcusable waste of money had he still been around.

On their tour of the building, Stephan pointed out its merits and deficiencies and introduced Courtney to several tenants, including a slick character named Brock Dicker whose "credit repair" company leased an entire floor, crammed with telemarketers pressuring the financially desperate and nearly bankrupt. During a brief chat, Courtney learned that Dicker and Patrick O'Malley were "good friends" and that both were members of Lakecrest Yacht Club. Though outwardly attentive and pleasant, Courtney felt troubled by the brief exchange. Dicker seemed a smooth operator, a grinning disingenuous hustler, not the kind of man she pictured Patrick befriending. She was also taken aback to learn that Patrick belonged to Lakecrest, an exclusive (some would say snooty) yacht club that cost tens of thousands of dollars just to join. She'd always imagined Patrick as more thrifty with his money, particularly with such a large family and several kids in college. From Stephan, Courtney learned that The Pinnacle had been fully leased for years, with no tenant turnover except for the floor leased to Brock Dicker six months earlier. Patrick had personally negotiated that deal, filling the space within a week of the previous tenant's departure.

The next day at the office, Patrick gave Courtney a condensed accounting of The Pinnacle's finances, disclosing a small operating loss over the preceding twelve months. Patrick pointed out, however, that the property actually had a positive cash flow if you took out depreciation from the balance sheet. While studying the numbers, Courtney offhandedly commented that the net revenues seemed low, considering the building was entirely leased. Patrick quickly explained that The Pinnacle had had some vacancies as well as some collection problems, not unusual for sub-prime commercial space. A tiny alarm went off in Courtney's head, because Stephan specifically had said occupancy had been stable for years. Though wondering about the inconsistency, Courtney instinctively kept it to herself. Changing the subject, she casually mentioned she'd met his "good friend" Brock Dicker during her visit.

Courtney Kossuth is one of those gifted few who can read people, who has an uncanny ability to decode nearly imperceptible facial expressions. Perhaps Pat's eyes widened slightly or perhaps his head recoiled a few centimeters. Whatever it was, Courtney instantly recognized Pat's discomfort hearing Dicker's name mentioned. Naturally, she wondered about that too. Later that day, she called Stephan Froelich who reaffirmed that The Pinnacle had been fully occupied for the last several years, that the floor occupied by Dicker had been vacant less than a month. Courtney then asked if Stephan knew of any tenants having problems paying their rent. Stephan did not know for sure, though he seriously doubted it, since Patrick never tolerated late payments. Like several other property managers, Stephan recounted how Patrick would occasionally direct him to confront tenants who fell behind in their rent. He hadn't had to perform this unpleasant task in almost a year.

All her instincts told Courtney that something was wrong, that Patrick was purposely deceiving her. She considered calling her father but decided to hold off until she had something more concrete to discuss with him. Even then, she worried about upsetting him. Feeble and now easily excitable, Tivadar Kossuth had never fully recovered from open-heart surgery over a year ago. Understandably, she was surprised when her upset father called her himself about an hour later. Apparently, Patrick had called Tivadar to tell him that Courtney had been meddling in his area of responsibility and undermining his authority at the company. According to Tivadar, Patrick had threatened to look for other work if she didn't become more of a team player. Too flabbergasted to respond effectively, Courtney weakly denied meddling and affirmed her desire to get along. She never mentioned her growing suspicions about Pat, fully expecting to be slammed if she did. Hanging up the phone, Courtney churned with feelings of betrayal and thought about quitting herself. But obviously that was what Uncle Patrick wanted! But why? So he could be CEO and run the company as he pleased? Possibly—maybe likely. But Pat's underhanded call to Courtney's father, with its baseless accusations and empty threats, suggested something more, something sinister.

Two days later, Patrick O'Malley fell from a ladder while retrieving water-skis stored in the rafters of his summer cottage's boathouse, breaking an elbow and two ribs, deflating a lung, and badly dislocating his shoulder. Both his injured elbow and shoulder required surgery. Patrick spent the next week in the hospital and two more weeks at home recuperating from his injuries, his first extended time off from work in ages. For the previous two years, he'd rarely taken a vacation, and never for more than a day or two at a time. His unfortunate accident proved fortunate for the Kossuth family, however, giving Courtney the undisturbed time to uncover Pat's self-dealing schemes and put an end to them.

Of course, the war must go on, even when a trusted officer goes down unexpectedly. Ever responsible, Courtney stepped up to help as best she could during Pat's absence. She resolved to learn as much as possible as quickly as possible and began by questioning the company controller, an older woman nearing retirement age named Irene. Loyal and unquestioning, Irene kept track of all company accounts excepting payroll. Despite having been with Fox Run Ltd. eleven years, Irene did not fully fathom the company's accounting system. She tried her best to allocate income and expenses to the appropriate project or property, but often relied on Patrick on how to book certain items. In other words, she obediently did whatever Patrick told her to do. The sheer magnitude of the business's many overlapping components complicated its accounting.

The company had more than $100 million in assets and debts that fluctuated between $40 and 50 million depending on projects underway. Money would often be moved from one account to another, depending on the capital and operational needs of the respective properties. Only Patrick completely understood what was going on financially with the company. Irene observed in passing, however, that gross profit margins seemed to have slipped, because the company now had to borrow short-term more frequently to meet current obligations, something that rarely happened when Tivadar managed the company.

Courtney sent flowers to Patrick at the hospital along with a "get well" card encouraging him not to worry while recuperating, telling him she'd make all the necessary arrangements to cover for him while absent. Upon receiving the note the day after his surgery, Patrick called Courtney from his hospital bed. Stupefied by painkillers and nearly incoherent, Patrick told her not to touch his work and to stay out of his files, mumbling his intention to return "in a few days." Sensing genuine anxiety behind his drug-induced disorientation, Courtney sweetly told Patrick to rest, get well, and not to fret about anything before she hung up the telephone.

Without hesitation, Courtney immediately went to Patrick's office and began snooping around. Finding several file cabinets and his desk drawers locked, she brought in a locksmith and had them opened. Meanwhile, Irene obligingly showed Courtney where Patrick filed the vendor and tenant contracts, various tax returns, and other data related to company operations. Courtney quickly found the tenant leases for The Pinnacle in a meticulously organized file cabinet containing company contracts. The agreements confirmed that the building had been fully leased for years. In fact, her father had signed every lease, except for the one with Dicker's "credit repair" firm, signed by Patrick just six months earlier. What troubled Courtney was that Dicker's monthly rate appeared to be substantially below market. According to the terms of the written agreement, Dicker paid even less rent than a tenant occupying just a third of the space on the floor below.

Courtney stayed long after everyone else had left for the day, looking through Patrick's accounting ledgers and files, all carefully kept and organized, though admittedly difficult for her to follow with her limited financial experience. Aware she needed help, she called a friend from her days with the symphony orchestra, a prominent businessman and trustee who'd headed the orchestra's audit committee. Without going into detail, Courtney confidentially told him she suspected some funny business and needed someone to help her get to the bottom of it. Her friend recommended a fraud investigator with considerable forensic accounting experience, a man who'd discreetly helped him with a similar problem at his own company not long before.

Investigation and Aftermath

The next day, Courtney met and engaged the investigator, who agreed to start immediately. To avoid activating the company rumor mill, Courtney introduced the man as an accountant who'd be filling in while Patrick recuperated. After that, Courtney mostly left him alone as he methodically reviewed the files, focusing first on The Pinnacle, his interest piqued by the aberrant lease agreement. The investigator quickly found other irregularities. According to company ledgers, certain tenants appeared to have missed some payments, yet checks received afterwards would be credited to the current month's rent rather than to the previous month's that apparently had been unpaid. Additionally, these delinquent accounts would periodically be reconciled to make them appear paid up. To anyone other than a fraud examiner, it made no sense whatsoever.

The investigator personally called five tenants whose accounts exhibited this inexplicable anomaly, identifying himself as a consultant undertaking a "routine" audit of Fox Run Ltd.'s books. He politely disclosed that company records indicated they were behind in their lease payments, some by as many as three months. Each tenant denied ever being late with the rent. The investigator responded by saying Fox Run's records said otherwise and apologetically asked each tenant to submit photocopies of all canceled rent checks (both front and back) for the last twelve months. He reassured them by saying that sloppy accounting on Fox Run's part was the likely explanation for the discrepancy. He also expressed his sincere thanks for their helping him correct the mistake.

While waiting for the canceled checks, the investigator carefully examined the contents of Patrick's computer, including its many archived email messages. Patrick had been lax about deleting them from his hard drive. Scores of emails indicated that Patrick not only had an investment interest in Brock Dicker's "credit repair" company but was also involved in its management. Furthermore, Patrick seemed to have had cozy relationships with several vendors, including the snow removal firm that Stephan Froelich had thought unnecessary. The investigator later discovered that the snow removal contractor was Patrick's wife's sister's husband. Other emails revealed that Patrick had also been handling lots of personal business on company time, such as negotiating the purchase of a new SUV and custom speedboat just a month before his accident. The investigator later confirmed that Patrick had paid more than $60,000 in cash for them, not needing financing to close the deals. How Patrick had accumulated this much money would soon become clear.

During his second week reviewing the files, the investigator met with Courtney and told her he'd found "the smoking gun" implicating Patrick. With some theatricality, he spread out a dozen photocopied checks he'd received that morning from one of The Pinnacle's tenants. Courtney looked at them quickly but nothing appeared unusual. The investigator suggested she look more closely at the deposit information on the back of the checks. The deposit stamp of one was similar but not identical to the remainder, differing only in the payee account number. The investigator then flipped that check over and asked Courtney to examine it carefully. Almost instantly she saw that the payee name "Fox Run Ltd." had been cleverly altered to "Fox Ran Ltd." The investigator then informed Courtney that "Fox Ran Ltd. was a relatively new corporation begun just the year before. The Secretary of State's records listed Patrick's wife, under her maiden name, as both the statutory agent and sole incorporator. State records also identified the company's address as a post office box at a postal branch just a few blocks from Patrick O'Malley's home.

Relatively quickly, the investigator found hard evidence that almost $200,000 had been diverted to Fox Ran Ltd. over the previous year and a half. He also found lots of circumstantial evidence suggesting Patrick had been receiving kickbacks from various vendors. For example, Patrick recently had approved a purchase order for twenty new air conditioning units at full retail price, even though Fox Run had received a proposal from another vendor for the same units discounted by 25 percent. Why would any responsible businessperson pay 25 percent more than necessary?

Courtney spent the next week working with the investigator and meeting privately with a few trusted advisers, including a respected attorney without previous ties with the company. Patrick called her twice during this time. Courtney never let on that she knew about his misconduct and instead pretended to look forward to his return, acting friendly and cheerfully clueless. The professionals advising her suggested lots of options, but ultimately Courtney alone decided what to do. Tempered by compassion and toughened by conviction, she acted swiftly and decisively. In short, she behaved like a seasoned business executive assuredly fixing a vexing problem.

Thin and pale, Patrick returned to work three weeks to the day following his accident. The receptionist steered him to the conference room, where he found Courtney waiting for him, flanked by the investigator and the attorney who'd helped advise her. Courtney would later say she surprised herself handling his firing so confidently, considering her intense emotions at the time. In a strong and even voice, Courtney confronted Patrick and succinctly disclosed what they'd discovered about his schemes. Then, genuinely interested, she asked him why he'd done it.

With face reddening, Patrick's demeanor shifted from perplexity to impotent anger, an expectable reaction for a cornered rat. Then with shocking bluntness, he blurted he'd taken the money because he was "owed" it, that he'd contributed mightily to the company's success but had never been adequately recognized or compensated for his years of selfless service. His resentment came out in an angry torrent toward Tivadar Kossuth ("that greedy cheapskate") and his children ("his coddled brats"). With hands folded, Courtney never interrupted and spoke only after Patrick wound down, his defiance dissipating to a fizzle, probably as a result of knowing that his goose was thoroughly cooked.

Courtney calmly told him his services were no longer needed. Then, looking at him squarely, she asked him to do two things. First, she wanted Patrick, in her presence, to call her father in Florida to tell him he'd decided to resign to pursue other opportunities and to thank him for his years of employment. Secondly, she wanted him to persuade Dicker and his "credit repair" firm to vacate The Pinnacle within thirty days, the lease nullified by mutual written agreement. If Patrick did both, Fox Run Ltd. would neither notify the authorities nor bring any legal action to recover what he'd misappropriated. The money would be treated as his severance payment, contingent of course upon his complete cooperation correcting the company's books. Courtney then told Patrick to go home to think about it, giving him just twenty-four hours to make his decision.

Early the next morning, Patrick called and accepted Courtney's offer in a shaky voice, probably terrified she'd change her mind and lower the boom on his guilty head. Within a week, Dicker's company found more spacious (and costly) offices on the other side of town and speedily packed up and left The Pinnacle. Patrick kept his word and called Tivadar Kossuth. In Courtney's presence, he told Tivadar about his resignation and thanked Tivadar for everything, authentically choking up during the conversation. To Courtney's surprise, he also told Tivadar that everything would be fine in Courtney's capable hands, that she had already demonstrated considerable aptitude and skill managing the company's affairs.

Following Patrick's departure and after a national search, Courtney hired an experienced CFO who totally revamped the company's accounting department, instituting various financial controls suggested by the fraud examiner. Last year, Fox Run Ltd. had record profitability under Courtney's leadership and also broke ground on a new condominium project. Some local business leaders have approvingly commented how much she reminds them of her father.

□ □ □ **COMMENTARY AND ANALYSIS**

In most ways other than its outcome, this case represents a fairly typical instance of business embezzlement. What makes it somewhat unusual is that Patrick got caught. Embezzlers rarely get caught and the cleverest ones almost never do, unnoticed by oblivious managers who create the opportunity and often the motivation behind employee thievery. A huge and growing problem, embezzlement ranks as the number-one financial crime according to FBI statistics, a position it's held for more than thirty years of FBI record-keeping.

Actual losses due to embezzlement and other forms of employee theft cannot be calculated precisely. The Association of Certified Fraud Examiners (ACFE), however, estimates losses to business as high as $600 billion per year, a staggering sum with a devastating impact on thousands of companies and investors. Losses from occupational fraud and abuse (the technical term, as defined by the ACFE, for using one's employment position for personal enrichment through the deliberate misuse or misapplication of the employing organization's resources or assets) constitute a serious drag on the health of our entire economy. In its 2003 *Report to the Nation,* the ACFE estimates organizations on average lose 6 percent of revenues to all forms of occupational fraud and abuse, losses that often represent the difference between success and failure. According to the ACFE, employee embezzlement and other misconduct may cause as many as a third of all business failures—outcomes that could be avoided through the use of proper financial controls and management practices.

There are thousands of ways for an employee to steal assets from an employer, and the criminally minded think up new ones every year. Patrick's diversion of company income represents just one common scheme perpetrated by dishonest employees. Other widespread methods include kickbacks, false sales, bid rigging, fictitious billings, check tampering, false claims, fictitious expenses, and a host of others. Catching perpetrators usually requires some luck. Probably less than 10 percent of asset misappropriations get discovered, and probably less than 10 percent of these ever get reported to the authorities. As a consequence, the problem vastly exceeds what criminal indictments and SEC disclosures would seem to indicate.

As a rule, the costliest embezzlements are executed not by career felons with shifty eyes and sticky fingers but by trusted older managers with college degrees and clean criminal records. The culprits are usually the last people you'd expect—which is why their embezzlements often continue for years without being detected. Most embezzlers, like Patrick, do not start their business careers aspiring to become thieves. They usually devolve into criminality slowly, tempted by opportunity and pressured by financial need or simple avarice. Embezzlers usually start small but eventually their thievery becomes more daring, emboldened by their avoiding detection. Given time and human nature, small embezzlements almost always grow into bigger ones.

All fraud investigators begin their training by learning about the fraud triangle: the three elements found in almost every case that motivate and allow people to commit fraud. The three elements are:

1. pressure to commit fraud;
2. rationalization or justification for the fraud;
3. the opportunity to commit and conceal the fraud;

Patrick O'Malley's financial misdeeds featured all three elements, a typical fraud scenario that illustrates why businesses should always have strong preventative measures in place.

Perpetrators always feel pressure, usually financial pressure, before committing fraud. Patrick O'Malley's case is just one demonstration of why an individual's high personal income does not necessarily mean he doesn't feel financial pressure. Patrick earned a six-figure salary but still felt pressured by the demands of supporting a large family with three children in college, another child with special needs, and a lavish lifestyle unsustainable on his earned income. For whatever reason, Patrick was the sort of individual whose ego (maybe his entire sense of self-worth) compelled him to flaunt and ultimately exaggerate his personal success. As an investigator, I have learned never to assume wealth when observing the trappings of wealth. Such trappings can be deceptive and even at times an indicator of financial mischief. In Patrick's case, the fraud examiner could have ignored the company ledgers and simply analyzed his personal assets and expenditures to see that something was amiss, that his lifestyle required resources well beyond his salary. Patrick owned more and spent more than his earnings should have permitted.

Financial concerns are not the only pressures that can motivate employees to steal from employers. Personal vices can exert strong pressures on people to commit fraud. Gamblers and drug addicts will often steal without hesitation to support their habits. If willing to burglarize a neighbor's home, drug addicts almost surely will look for ways to steal from their employers. Work-related pressures also can lead to fraud. When provoked by an extremely callous or cruel boss, hate can be a powerful motivator for "revenge fraud." Some embittered employees like Patrick will try to even the score for being overworked, underpaid, overlooked, or undervalued. Job dissatisfaction or fear of losing a job may also pressure some employees to scheme and steal.

Without pressure—financial or otherwise—fraud will seldom occur. Unfortunately, our money-worshipping culture now creates pressures that are pervasive and unremitting, encouraging people to steal to get ahead. The growing problem of fraud in the workplace is at least in part the consequence of our society, which too often measures success by money and wealth. Too many people today value financial success above honesty and integrity, above goodness and generosity. Many now seem to have trouble differentiating between want and need. We have become a fretful society driven by rising desires and outlandish expectations, a collection of anxious souls with incessant longings, more aware of what we lack than what we have. Patrick O'Malley was not at all unusual in his craving for more and more. With the conventional cultural controls of morality and rectitude waning, businesses must become ever more vigilant in protecting their assets, or face the consequences of culturally driven greed.

At least to themselves, perpetrators always try to rationalize or justify their actions before committing fraud, a key element in the fraud triangle. Patrick O'Malley undoubtedly had been brooding long before committing fraud, growing more resentful as the Kossuth family grew wealthier while he got tossed crumbs by comparison. Like most disgruntled employees, he had an inflated sense of his own importance and contributions, sincerely believing he'd been responsible for much (if not most) of the company's success. Diverting company income to his personal use was, in his mind, merely well-deserved compensation, his fair share of the profits he'd helped generate. He perceived that the Kossuth family had been exploiting him for years. Taking checks from the company was simply his way to right a wrong.

Besides the "I deserve it" excuse, perpetrators commonly rationalize their misconduct by telling themselves that they're only "borrowing" the money, fully intending to pay it back someday. When I first started out as an investigator many years ago, fraudsters generally would be contrite when exposed and would earnestly plead for forgiveness and understanding, claiming they'd always intended to pay back "every last dime." Nowadays, fraud examiners hear remorse less often when confronting perpetrators, who now will shrug indifferently and say things like, "You caught me, so what," unashamed of what they've done. I find this unrepentant attitude chilling, an indicator that our society may have lost its bearings in this rising storm of cultural greed.

In addition to unbridled greed, widespread fear of an uncertain future may also be pushing ostensibly upright people into embezzlement. Not many decades ago, hard-working and dependable employees could count on secure futures with stable jobs that provided adequate health-care and retirement benefits. Those days are gone, replaced by growing uncertainties and worries for even the most responsible, capable, and highly trained workers. Traditional pensions with defined benefits have been replaced by skimpy 401(k) plans that for most will be woefully inadequate at providing a comfortable, worry-free retirement. Health-care benefits have been slashed, eliminated, or shifted to the workers under co-pay arrangements. Venerable manufacturing companies, even whole industries, have closed or downsized. The Social Security system seems destined to collapse under the weight of an aging population. In today's cutthroat economy, loyalty has become as outmoded as chivalry, a quaint vestige from the days of handshake business deals.

Small wonder that more and more people consider feathering their own nest by misappropriating their employers' assets, particularly when the odds of getting caught are slim and the odds of getting punished even slimmer. The risks of fraud will grow as our culture devolves further into an "every man for himself" scramble, and the security implications for business will be profound in the future. After all, even the saintly would consider committing fraud to avoid living in a cardboard box under a highway overpass.

Faced with increasing societal pressures coupled with easy rationalizations, organizations must try to eliminate every opportunity for employees to commit fraud (the third element of the fraud triangle) in order to control the risks. The most financially pressured employee, encouraged by airtight rationalizations, will not commit fraud if never presented the opportunity. On the flip side, I believe that every opportunity found to commit fraud will eventually be exploited; the only question is when.

After heart disease forced Tivadar Kossuth to retire, Patrick O'Malley found himself with almost unlimited opportunities to steal from the company. Tivadar's presence had previously been an effective control. Obsessively involved in every aspect of the business, Tivadar would almost certainly have detected any financial improprieties on his watch. In fact, the fraud investigator found no evidence that Patrick had taken anything prior to Tivadar's illness. Quite likely, Patrick never even thought about diverting company checks to himself, knowing full well he'd have been caught had he done so. Patrick's scheming began in earnest only after it became clear Tivadar would not return, his departure creating the both opportunity and the justification for Patrick's fraud. Tivadar's bypassing Patrick as his permanent replacement and naming the less-qualified Courtney instead undoubtedly represented the final affront that drove him to plunder company assets.

Eliminating opportunities for asset misappropriation requires having in place the right financial controls and business practices, which by design make it difficult for a perpetrator to escape detection. Embezzlers like Patrick must have more than simply the opportunity to steal; they must also believe they can successfully conceal their crimes. The stronger their sense that their schemes will be detected, the less likely it is that they will ever attempt them. In this sense, fraud perpetrators are much easier to thwart than hardened street felons, criminals driven more by impulse and passion. Fraudsters are calculating and deliberate offenders, who carefully weigh the potential benefits against the risks of getting caught. Their threat can be controlled by increasing the risks of detection and limiting the potential rewards of misconduct.

The most basic yet effective financial control is simply to separate a company's money from its record-keeping function. To that end, it is essential to separate the accounts receivable from the banking functions. Of course, receipts and deposits should balance each day, and different employees should tally and track each. After Patrick's departure, Fox Run Ltd. changed the operations of its finance department. One employee would receive, log, and total the daily receipts, then a second employee would prepare the deposit, and lastly the CFO would verify that the totals balanced before personally making the deposit.

Another financial control entails separating the accounts payable from the procurement functions, effective when combined with a strict approval process requiring supporting documentation whenever changing or adding vendors. One individual (or department) should approve and process payments, another should prepare and send checks, and a third should reconcile bank accounts. In fact, the three functions every business owner should always segregate (or do himself) are 1) writing checks, 2) making bank deposits, and 3) reconciling bank statements. An axiom of fraud deterrence is that no employee, no matter how senior or trusted, should ever have complete control over an entire transaction. This separation of duties is one of the first and most effective things any business can do to prevent fraud.

Other financial controls can help thwart employee fraud and abuse. Dual custody, for example, prevents a single employee from having complete authority over a transaction. Dual custody requires two employees to collaborate on a task, such as signing checks. Dual custody and separation of duties both have the same purpose: preventing one person from having unchecked access to organizational funds. Implementing a system of authorizations is another effective control. When an employee is not authorized for a certain duty, the opportunity to commit fraud can be reduced significantly. For example, if an employee has no authorization to approve purchases, he will be unable to order items for his personal use and have the company pay for them.

Independent checks and surprise audits also serve as deterrents to occupational fraud and abuse. If employees know that others will monitor their work, the opportunity to commit or conceal their fraud will be reduced or even eliminated. Periodic job rotations, preferably unannounced, similarly deter employee mischief. As a matter of policy, all employees should be required to take vacations—not a day here or there, but extended time off during which their duties will be handled by another. Many frauds (such as Patrick's) are uncovered when perpetrators are unexpectedly absent from work, powerless to cover the tracks of their scheming. During employees' vacations or lengthy medical leaves of absence, work should never be permitted to pile up. Knowledgeable substitutes should always step in and handle their assignments without interruption. Besides deterring occupational fraud and abuse, using capable alternates who thoroughly understand the job function makes good business sense, because life is unpredictable. The most indispensable employee might get hit by a bus tomorrow, and businesses must always be prepared for that very real possibility.

Monitoring employees and their work product is of course the cornerstone of fraud deterrence, but how this is done requires sensitivity and understanding. Financial controls and fraud prevention measures should never be unveiled as "stopping fraud," implying the workforce is untrustworthy. Concern for theft must be conveyed without creating a climate of distrust and paranoia, which can hurt morale and cause employee turnover. Management should instead remind the workforce that organizational success comes from collaboration, with employees relying on one another, catching and correcting each other's mistakes, and helping each other for the greater good of the organization. In healthy work environments, colleagues watch each others' backs rather than breathe down each others' necks. In short, employees should never feel suspected and distrusted; they should feel engaged and entrusted as active participants in the success of the organization.

To that end, every organization should have employee suggestion boxes or hot lines, giving the workforce the opportunity to recommend improvements, to share operational insights, and to report problems and suspicions. People are often reluctant to report suspected wrongdoing directly to management but will readily do so anonymously. According to the ACFE, anonymous tips expose more cases of occupational fraud than do the efforts of canny auditors.

Promoting and sustaining an ethical culture is just as important as having strong financial controls when it comes to combating occupational fraud and abuse. Every organization should draft and ratify an ethics policy, clearly declaring an expectation of ethical behavior and compliance with all applicable laws and regulations. Formal written policies do indeed make a difference. Companies with strong policies against absenteeism, for example, have less of a problem with absenteeism than those without them. Similarly, a strong ethics policy can help prevent employee misconduct. An ethics policy should be more than just an "everyone must be good" statement. An ethics policy should list specific conduct that violates the policy, disclose the disciplinary consequences for violating the policy, and outline a mechanism for reporting unethical conduct.

Needless to say, an ethics policy must be followed and enforced, modeled by the highest levels of management to set the tone for the entire organization. If senior management acts like a rapacious pack of thieves plundering customers and company alike, an ethics policy will mean next to nothing. As every parent knows, "do what I say, not what I do" will never be heeded by subordinates. To be effectual, words must always conform with actions.

Some years back, I was involved in a case where a senior manager got caught covertly providing a competitor, presumably for personal benefit, proprietary information on a key production process. His betrayal shocked and outraged company officials, but in fact they shouldn't have been surprised by his misconduct. During the investigation, it came out that these same officials had hired this person partly because he brought with him helpful proprietary information from his prior employer, which he'd secretly photocopied and filched just before he resigned. Now, why would these officials be surprised he'd done to them what they knew he'd done before to others? In business, I believe companies that countenance thievery will eventually be victimized by theft. Prudent managers should always shun job applicants who come bearing questionable gifts, since whatever the unscrupulous bring in through the door will inevitably go out through the window.

I am often unmoved by the righteous indignation of the victims of fraud, business owners and managers who turn purple with rage upon discovering their losses and the treachery of a trusted employee. More often than not, these outraged dupes were complicit, having made it easy for the thefts to occur. Frankly, they should look themselves in the mirror when ascribing blame. Business owners and managers have a moral (not just fiduciary) obligation to eliminate all obvious opportunities for occupational fraud and abuse.

Decades ago in Sunday School, I learned the pious should always avoid "near occasions of sin," temptations to do something wrong. I also learned that creating a "near occasion of sin," tempting others to do something wrong, was in itself sinful. I took this lesson to heart and believe strongly that those business owners and managers who fail to establish effective financial and operational controls, and thus create or allow opportunities for occupational fraud and abuse, are almost as guilty as the offenders who take advantage of them. Should we really feel sorry for the person who, figuratively speaking, leaves the money drawer open and later finds it empty? Does this dullard deserve our sympathy or our derision? Over the years, I have seen many weak people give in to temptation, ordinary souls who might have toiled to retirement without taking a thumbtack had proper controls been in place. The sad outcomes of certain cases sometimes bothered me. I cannot help thinking various offenders might easily have received a gold watch instead of a pink slip or (in some cases) a criminal indictment had their bosses just eliminated blatant opportunities to misappropriate assets.

Don't misunderstand: I believe offenders should always face consequences for their misconduct, but that doesn't always mean throwing the book at someone, seeking criminal penalties to the maximum extent of the law. Courtney Kossuth obviously felt the same way. Caught red-handed, Patrick O'Malley almost surely would have been indicted and convicted on felony charges had the authorities been notified. Would that have been the more fitting outcome? Did Courtney shirk her civic duty by letting Patrick go and treating his theft as compensation? To be honest, I have mixed feelings about her handling of him, but I understand why Courtney did what she did. Courtney intuitively knew her family was far from blameless under the circumstances. In truth, Tivadar had substantially underpaid Patrick O'Malley considering his responsibilities and the pay-scale for senior executives in the region. Did this excuse Patrick's misconduct? Obviously not, but it certainly made his conduct more understandable. He is an example that inequitable treatment often provokes employee fraud and abuse. Conversely, fairness (or better yet generosity) counteracts the same.

Courtney also recognized that Fox Run Ltd. and her family, in addition to Patrick, would face consequences had she called the authorities and reported his thievery. Her father would have been rocked by the disclosure and would certainly have been called as a witness. Courtney refused to subject him to such strain, which might have been fatal considering his fragile health. Courtney also understood that the company would have been roiled by a criminal investigation, demoralizing and distracting the workforce, creating a public-

ASSET MISAPPROPRIATION IN THE WORKPLACE □ 141

relations nightmare that would have consumed time and energy. Some hard-liners might argue that Courtney missed a valuable opportunity to make Patrick an example by prosecuting him, reminding other employees that thievery would always be severely punished, thereby thwarting future employee misconduct. Though I understand the argument, I personally believe (like Courtney) that the negative consequences of pursuing an indictment would have outweighed the positive ones in this particular case. Implementing preventative controls was far more effective and much less disruptive than sending a man to prison. Most companies with similar issues conclude the same and choose to deal quietly with employee misconduct, usually by firing offenders and foregoing the criminal justice system. Is this a good thing from a public policy perspective? Probably not, but given the complexities and concerns of business today, it is certainly the easier route to take.

The size of the misappropriation often compels owners and managers to involve the authorities. Though not much money for the Kossuth family, $200,000 in losses for many businesses is a considerable sum, well worth recovery efforts. Unfortunately, the authorities and the criminal courts are not particularly helpful in this regard. Victimized companies should seriously consider obtaining a civil judgment against the perpetrator for the losses, irrespective of the criminal court's directive that the stolen funds be repaid, usually over time. I have seen a number of cases where offenders steal hundreds of thousands of dollars, serve a very short sentence, and then return to the good life, making small monthly payments towards an obligation that will take decades (sometimes centuries) to fulfill. On more than a few occasions, I have seen these same offenders subsequently come into a lot of money, through inheritances for example, enough to make the victimized company whole. Under no obligation to pay more than the court-ordered monthly sum, they can thumb their noses at their former employers if the statute of limitations for a civil suit has expired. Had these victimized companies obtained a civil judgment after the criminal trials, usually a relatively simple matter, they could have gone after those subsequently acquired assets.

Fraud prevention is always better (and much easier) than fraud detection. Uncovering occupational fraud and abuse can be enormously difficult and costly. Skilled investigators are rare, and even the best cannot avoid the tedious, time-consuming steps required to unravel complex fraud schemes. Think of auditors as watchdogs and fraud examiners as bloodhounds. Bloodhounds almost never travel in straight lines; they instead wander in circles trying to pick up and follow the scent. I have seen cases take months and even years to complete. Courtney expedited the process by pointing the investigator in fruitful directions, thereby avoiding what could have been a lengthy and enormously expensive examination. Most occupational-fraud investigations do not come together so easily.

Courtney Kossuth handled a challenging and consequential problem remarkably well considering her inexperience, demonstrating an intuitive alertness all business owners and managers should emulate. People should always be attentive to what others say and do, alert to the red flags that may indicate something is wrong. Stonewalling and incomplete or evasive answers by subordinates to straightforward questions should always be treated with suspicion. Courtney quite rightly found Patrick's unresponsiveness to her financial queries cause for concern. She also took immediate notice when his explanation in regard to The Pinnacle's mediocre financial performance made little sense.

Furthermore, Courtney rightly wondered about Patrick's extravagant personal expenditures. Owners and managers should be alert to sudden, inexplicable lifestyle changes, such as a middle manager earning $50,000 per year who buys a $50,000 Lexus. Always be suspicious of the "inheritance" explanation. Offenders frequently use a recent "bequest" to explain how they can afford newly acquired luxuries, and most listeners naively accept this explanation despite its improbability. How many readers have an aunt or uncle who'd leave them any money, let alone a large sum?

From my professional experience, I've learned automatically to distrust improbable explanations. When suspecting employee misconduct, I encourage owners and managers to trust their instincts and intuitions. Do not ignore gut feelings or stifle them by intellectually reaching for explanations. Our intuitions rarely fail us, but our intellects often do, second-guessing or countermanding what we already intuitively know to be true. When intuiting something disturbing, try to resist thinking "there has to be another explanation." This is particularly important in regard to negative instincts about people. Courtney immediately (and correctly) sensed Brock Dicker was untrustworthy, and thus that Patrick O'Malley was suspect by association. My wife's grandmother (God rest her soul) often said, "Show me your friends and I'll show you who you are." From my professional perspective, truer words were never said.

□ □ □ **CAUTIONARY TIPS:**

- There are no small frauds, just little ones waiting to grow into big ones.
- Financial controls are cheaper than fraud detection.
- Fairness and generosity combat asset misappropriation, while greed and selfishness promote it.

CHAPTER 7

Sexual Harassment Lawsuits

□ □ □ **CASE #1—HAROLD TUPPER:**
   "YOU TOUCH IT, YOU BOUGHT IT"

Harold Tupper was the wealthy owner of a manufacturing company in a conservative Midwest suburb. Though basically a well-meaning person, Harold tended to alienate those around him with his morose personality. Subordinates often mistook his natural reserve for coldness and condescension. Harold's sour disposition, however, had less to do with the pressures of business than with problems at home. His wife of twenty years, depending on her mood, daily threatened him with either divorce or suicide, and unfairly blamed him for everything in her miserable life. Their marriage amounted to nothing more than a shared loathing. Understandably, Harold had become increasingly tense and distracted at work.

One Monday morning, Harold's very capable secretary quit without notice or explanation. For months, she had misinterpreted his black moods as evidence of his dissatisfaction with her work. Finally, she could take it no longer. For Harold, her sudden resignation came as a complete shock, leaving him frantic and even more despondent. In reality, he had completely relied upon her and never once questioned her competence. Replacing her became an urgent priority for Harold, already nearing emotional overload, making him even more vulnerable for the coming debacle.

Harold Tupper personally interviewed several promising candidates and quickly settled on one. Theresa Ivory seemed qualified for the position. According to her résumé, she had worked for two years as an "administrative assistant" for a small electronics company that had gone out of business. Her prior boss, according to Theresa, "retired either to Florida or Arizona," she wasn't quite sure which. When Harold asked about her extended unemployment following her layoff, Theresa told him a heartbreaking story about caring for her mother,

□ 145

who had recently died from cancer. A cursory background check confirmed she had earned an associate degree from a local business college. During her interview, Harold couldn't help gaping at her. Theresa was simply gorgeous. She also had a sparkling personality, relaxed and cheerful yet poised and professional. As smitten as teenager, Harold hired her on the spot.

Within a week, Theresa had become indispensable, revamping the filing system and quickly accomplishing every task she was assigned. Her cheerfulness dispelled Harold's gloom and he actually felt light-hearted for the first time in memory. He so enjoyed her sunny disposition that he contrived reasons to speak with her, adding new responsibilities that often kept her around after business hours. She never complained. After a few weeks, he thought they were becoming friends. Time spent with Theresa awakened Harold to life's possibilities, and he began fantasizing about divorcing his wife and starting anew. When Harold dropped hints about his unhappy marriage, Theresa responded sympathetically, expressing disbelief that his wife could be so cold to someone so "kind and special." Rather shyly, she alluded to her own romantic disappointments.

Harold remembered the first time he touched her. Self-consciously, he gently rested his hand on her shoulder while watching her scroll through the financial report on her monitor. His heart fluttered wildly when she reached up and briefly patted his hand, her eyes never leaving the computer screen in front of her. Lightheaded with desire, Harold swooned back into his office, incapable of speaking for some minutes. Emboldened, he later complimented her on her excellent work and impulsively hugged her. She did not resist.

Soon, Harold was confiding the sad details of his failed marriage and hinting at his attraction for her. Theresa blushed coyly and admitted she was "very flattered." Like an old friend, Theresa listened attentively but shared little about herself. One day, Harold invited her to lunch at an elegant nearby restaurant, resolved to state his feelings for her. She accepted enthusiastically.

This lunch date became the most baffling experience of Harold's life. After two glasses of wine, he stammered out his feelings for her. She responded in monosyllables and her voice seemed oddly flat, though she smiled sweetly and frequently squeezed his hand whenever he said something heartfelt. While waiting for the check, he awkwardly propositioned her. She smiled again, gently stroked his cheek with her fingertips, but answered coldly, "I don't think so."

After lunch, Theresa told Harold that she wasn't feeling well and went home early. She never returned to work again. Harold tried calling her at home several times but always got her answering machine. He left three increasingly mawkish messages that he later knew were a mistake. Theresa never returned his calls. When he called a fourth time, after Theresa had been absent for a week, Harold discovered that her telephone was no longer in service.

About three weeks later, a deputy sheriff served him with the complaint. The plaintiff, Theresa Ivory, was suing Harold and his company for sexual harassment, a hostile work environment, intentional infliction of emotional distress, and constructive discharge. In support of the allegations, paragraph six of the complaint referred to his messages on her home answering machine and also to a secretly recorded tape of their luncheon conversation. The plaintiff sought $1 million in compensatory and punitive damages. The plaintiff also asked the court to issue a restraining order prohibiting the defendant from "contacting, stalking, harassing, or otherwise menacing" the plaintiff.

Investigation and Aftermath

In the months that followed, Harold's life collapsed around him. Several key employees left the company. After learning of the lawsuit, Harold's wife filed for divorce and began to lay siege to both the company and the marital assets. Her attorney petitioned the court for an expedited discovery schedule, claiming that Harold's "mismanagement" jeopardized the value of her dower interests. Meanwhile, Harold's attorney, a jovial backslapper from a large firm, spent considerable time on Harold's problems, quickly billing him more than $40,000 for "legal research" and "case management." During a most friendly and optimistic telephone conference, he requested an additional $50,000 retainer before taking depositions in what he called "the Theresa Ivory matter."

Deeply humiliated, and tortured by self-incrimination, Harold Tupper devolved into a paralyzed husk of his formerly capable self. His emotional low point came when he discovered a Post-it note stuck to the wall in the executive bathroom with a sketch of a naked man chasing a clothed woman. Underneath the crude drawing was the caption:

Harold Tupper
Tried to boink her
But Theresa ran
Before he can!

A dark, swarming sensation seemed to constrict his heart as Harold ripped the offending note into tiny pieces and flushed them down the toilet. Later that afternoon, he met with his attorney and spent the first five minutes sobbing and wringing the life out of his case folder. After calming down enough to speak, Harold sputtered out his suspicions, previously kept to himself, that Theresa Ivory's lawsuit was nothing more an elaborate shakedown. He demanded that she be investigated. Peering over the top of his glasses, his attorney reluctantly agreed to hire an investigator. He warned Harold, however, that it could go against him if discovered by the other side, potentially adding an invasion of privacy claim to his already considerable legal problems. Harold agreed to accept that risk, which his attorney promptly confirmed in writing the next day.

An experienced private investigator began a discreet inquiry into Theresa Ivory's past with a simple computer search and quickly discovered suspicious information, including fourteen different addresses and several aliases associated with her name over the previous four years. Three Social Security numbers were linked to her, along with six judgments for unpaid bills. Curiously, Theresa had moved shortly after filing the lawsuit against Harold and left no forwarding address. Her former landlord knew nothing about her whereabouts and asked to be kept informed, explaining that she still owed him money. Theresa's attorney, whose specialty was actually criminal defense, offered no explanation, saying only that Theresa was perfectly safe and receiving intensive therapy from a psychologist for "post-traumatic stress syndrome."

In certain difficult cases, the most helpful witness is often a former spouse, preferably an embittered one. Records indicated that Theresa had divorced her husband, a salesman at a local Cadillac dealership. When contacted by the investigator, Theresa's ex-husband began the conversation by asking, "What's that bitch done now?" Her ex-husband revealed that Theresa made her living mostly as an "entertainer" at various gentlemen's clubs. Two years before, she had hooked up with the owner of one of these places, working as his part-time personal assistant by day and as a stripper by night. Her ex-husband had also heard that the man had recently sold the club and opened another in a Gulf Coast resort town. Apparently, Theresa had briefly broken up with him, which had necessitated her taking the job at Harold's company, though her ex had heard that they were back together again. Presumably she was with him down south. Theresa's ex-husband also told the investigator that, contrary to Theresa's sad story, her mother was alive and well. Patrons of two local clubs confirmed that Theresa was in fact an extremely accomplished and popular "entertainer."

According to other reliable sources, shaking down businessmen had become a cottage industry for some of her dancer colleagues. After a night of frivolity, they would file charges of sexual assault with the police, their cases supported by vaginal swabs and tearful accounts recorded on emergency-room intake forms. After being paid handsomely for their silence, the "victims" would refuse to testify. Charges would then be dropped against the businessmen.

The investigator traced Theresa and her boyfriend to a tacky beach-front community, where she was already a local favorite, having added the famed Texas Couch Dance to her repertoire. The investigator, posing as a customer, documented her superior dancing skills with a pinhole video camera concealed in a fanny pack. Upon receipt of the videotape, Harold's attorney was so impressed by its production values that he replayed it several times behind closed doors.

At a pretrial conference, Theresa Ivory's attorney made an impassioned pitch for a substantial settlement, arguing his client had been seriously "scarred" by Harold's unwelcome sexual advances. In response, Harold's attorney played the videotape and afterward said sarcastically, "I didn't see any scars." Unflustered and seemingly unconcerned by the videotape, Theresa's attorney countered by saying the videotape was immaterial and repeated his demand for a substantial settlement. With a scornful laugh, Harold's attorney closed his briefcase with a flourish and swaggered from the room.

The next month, Theresa's attorney deposed Harold, a brutal six-hour ordeal that left him feeling utterly humiliated and violated. Besides admitting his physical attraction to Theresa, he was forced to describe in embarrassing detail his sexual habits and marital problems. Theresa's attorney even asked about his early toilet training, suggesting some perverse and long-standing psychological disorder. Agitated and stammering throughout, Harold acknowledged under oath that Theresa had rebuffed his sexual advances.

At her deposition soon thereafter, Theresa wore a gold crucifix and remained perfectly composed for three hours, answering frankly all questions concerning her part-time career as a "dancer." She vehemently denied ever saying she'd cared for her "dying" mother, calling Harold a liar and a lecher. She testified that "dancing" was her "craft," which she hoped would lead to a Hollywood career someday. Theresa said Harold knew all about her dancing and, on the basis of that knowledge, obviously made some wrong assumptions about her moral character.

After the depositions, Harold's attorney filed a motion for summary judgment that was promptly denied. At this point, Harold's legal bills already exceeded $100,000. A half-year later, and just weeks before trial, Theresa's attorney filed a motion *in limine* (a pretrial motion requesting the court to prohibit opposing counsel from referring to or offering evidence on especially prejudicial matters) petitioning the court to exclude the videotape from the trial, arguing that the danger of prejudice substantially outweighed the probative value of the tape's admission into evidence. The court granted the motion and issued a protective order restricting the defendant and his legal counsel from "mentioning, referring to, or attempting to convey to the jury in any manner, either directly or indirectly, anything related to the plaintiff's sex life, sexual nature, or personal character."

The day before trial and on the advice of legal counsel, Harold agreed to pay Theresa $150,000 to settle the lawsuit. Six months later, he put his company up for sale; his wife had forced this move by refusing stock in the divorce settlement, wanting cash instead. The banks, concerned by the company's deteriorating balance sheet, would not loan him the money needed to buy out her dower interests. A multinational conglomerate subsequently bought the company below the price originally stipulated in the purchase contract, the amount being adjusted downward just before closing after an unusually contentious due-diligence investigation by the buyer. When threatened with a lawsuit for material misrepresentations and unspecified damages, Harold caved under the pressure and conceded to the purchaser's last-minute discount demands. Six months later, Harold was hospitalized for depression and various stress-related ailments.

□ □ □ **CASE #2—BILL TROST:**
"I ONLY HAVE EYES FOR YOU"

Bill Trost rebelled against the conventional business world with its starched shirts and red tape. Before starting his own computer software firm, Bill had worked unhappily for a Fortune 500 company, despising what he saw as the corporate obsession with policies and procedures that controlled every aspect of life on the job. He now wore scuffed tennis shoes and faded T-shirts to work. As a boss, character and capability impressed him, not appearances and pretense. He was unreservedly proud of the dozen scruffy eccentrics who comprised his loyal and hardworking staff.

The pretty new receptionist, Margaret Mary Semple, was unlike the brash, unkempt programmers already working for the company. Well groomed and well dressed, Margaret was also somewhat timid, even skittish, like a young doe nervously crossing a country road at dusk. A mother with two teenage children, Margaret had recently divorced her husband after learning he'd been unfaithful. This was the first job she'd held in almost fourteen years.

When Bill Trost introduced Margaret to her new coworkers, he noticed Robertson Hipple staring at her as if she were a piece of cake.

Shaped like a russet potato, Robertson was an introverted man who mostly kept to himself and rarely spoke to others. He was also a brilliant programmer, personally responsible for almost a third of the code written and released by the company. In hindsight, Bill Trost should have anticipated that Robertson's obvious attraction to Margaret might lead to serious problems.

When introduced, Robertson took Margaret's outstretched hand in both of his, grasping longer than etiquette dictates; this was possibly the first physical contact he'd had with a woman in years. After some uncomfortable moments, she twisted her hand free and tightly crossed her arms. Robertson failed to read her explicit body language. In the following weeks, Bill Trost frequently saw Robertson hanging around Margaret's desk, wide-eyed and expectant, like a dog waiting for a morsel. Rigid and uncommunicative, she tried her best to ignore his pitiful attempts to initiate conversation. Occasionally, she'd find presents left anonymously on her desk, such as candy and flowers, which she'd promptly transfer to the lunchroom for everyone's enjoyment.

After a month on the job, Margaret asked to speak with Bill Trost. Tears welling, she told her boss that Robertson's incessant and clumsy overtures were becoming unbearable. Despite her repeated and unambiguous refusals to date him, Robertson continued to ask her out. She disclosed she was very nervous around him, not because of anything threatening he'd said, but more because he was so strange, so devoid of social skills. Anxious and miserable, she wanted Bill to intervene and stop Robertson from badgering her further, which Trost agreed to do.

Trost immediately called Robertson into his office and patiently explained that Margaret felt uneasy around him and wanted her space. Becoming flustered and emotional, Robertson blurted out that he couldn't will his feelings to change, and that he felt humiliated that his pure intentions had been so misconstrued. He offered to resign— he felt that leaving was the only possible balm for his unrequited love. Robertson was obviously emotionally upended, but so was Bill at the prospect of losing his ace programmer.

Instantly changing directions, Bill put his hand on the programmer's shoulder and counseled him like a brother, bemoaning the heartlessness of women and encouraging him to be gentle with himself. He reassured Robertson that he had done nothing wrong, that the vagaries of love required patience and a thick skin. Bill encouraged him, however, to be less ardent with his solicitations and to back off. After the programmer left, Bill congratulated himself on the sympathetic and sensitive way he'd handled both employees.

Afterwards, Bill occasionally saw Robertson near Margaret but much less so than before his intervention. The bulbous programmer still occasionally left thoughtful treats on her desk, but scrupulously dispensed the same treats to others as well. Anyone could see that he was still smitten, though he mooned from a more respectful distance. About a month later, Margaret again asked to speak privately with Bill. More vehemently this time, she complained about Robertson's continuing attentions and again asked Bill to make him stop. She acknowledged that Robertson no longer asked her out, but he still circled her like a vulture, following her to the lunch room, leaving work at the same time, and constantly contriving reasons to speak with her. She had been losing weight and sleep worrying about his behavior.

Bill listened patiently but inwardly felt irritated. After she finished complaining, he shrugged his shoulders and said that there was little more he could do, that nothing she had recounted seemed offensive to him. He told her to relax. She should feel flattered, not offended. Flushed, Margaret responded that Robertson's attentions were unwelcome, adding that she had repeatedly and unambiguously conveyed this fact to him. She then insisted that Bill, as company owner, had to do something about the situation.

Even progressive bosses have their limits—and their blind spots. Bill coldly told her that he had a business to run and had neither the time nor the inclination to get involved in petty personality frictions. If she found her job so unpleasant, he said bluntly, perhaps she should think about working elsewhere. Margaret stared at him icily for some moments, then got up without another word and left the office. She never returned. Initially, Bill Trost felt much relieved. Margaret, in his opinion, had been too sensitive and, over time, might easily have driven away his most valuable employee.

Two weeks later, Bill Trost received a letter from an attorney with a legal complaint, as yet unfiled, in which the plaintiff, Margaret Semple, demanded unspecified monetary damages in excess of $100,000 for sexual harassment, intentional infliction of emotional distress, constructive discharge, and a hostile work environment. The attorney suggested that the matter could be settled quickly and quietly if good-faith negotiations commenced at once. In addition to the company, both Bill and Robertson Hipple were named personally as defendants in the complaint. Incensed, Bill immediately called his lawyer.

Investigation and Aftermath

After listening to Bill Trost rant about the absurdity of Margaret Semple's charges, the attorney patiently advised him that her allegations could have significant financial consequences if affirmed by the court. The attorney then recommended using a skilled investigator to interview company personnel to help assess the case and shape a defense. The next day, the investigator arrived and first interviewed Bill Trost. After reviewing certain background information, the investigator got to the important issues.

INVESTIGATOR: "Does your company have a written, well-publicized sexual harassment policy?"

TROST: "No."

INVESTIGATOR: "Does your company have a written, well-publicized procedure or avenue whereby employees can express concerns and complaints?"

TROST: "Nothing formal, but my door is always open. In fact, Margaret spoke with me

INVESTIGATOR: "Did she tell you she was being harassed by him?"

TROST: "She didn't use the word 'harassed' but she did complain about his attentions. But she was just being overly sensitive . . . Robertson did nothing but ask her out and bring her some candy."

INVESTIGATOR: "Did Robertson continue to ask her out after she turned him down?"

TROST: "Yes, at first . . . but he stopped after I spoke with him."

INVESTIGATOR: "So she asked you to intervene on her behalf?"

TROST: "Yes, and I did. After the first time she complained I spoke with Robertson and told him to back off and be less ardent."

INVESTIGATOR: "Did you explicitly tell him to stop all contact that was not work related?"

TROST: "No, but . . . hey, the guy had a crush on her, OK? He was harmless . . . she was making a mountain out of a molehill. Besides, I'm a businessman, not a social worker."

INVESTIGATOR: "Did she say that Mr. Hipple's flirtations were unwelcome?"

TROST: "Yes."

INVESTIGATOR: "Did Ms. Semple tell you that her physical or mental health were being affected by Mr. Hipple's unwelcome attentions?"

TROST: "She said she was losing weight and sleep . . . which was ridiculous. Robertson is harmless—just an awkward guy who happened to like her."

INVESTIGATOR: "So you did not take her complaints seriously?"

TROST: "To be honest, no, I did not . . . she was just being overly sensitive, which I told her in so many words."

INVESTIGATOR: "You did nothing then after she complained a second time?"

TROST: "I told her she should consider looking for another job, but I didn't fire her or ask her to resign. She left of her own accord. Look, how can there possibly be any basis to her charge of sexual harassment? Robertson wasn't her supervisor . . . there was no quid pro quo demand and no retaliation. Her accusations are ridiculous!"

Bill had the uncomfortable impression that the investigator was displeased with his answers. The investigator reminded Bill that his job was simply to gather facts. The company attorney would review the merits of Margaret's complaint after he had completed his inquiry.

After speaking with Bill, the investigator interviewed two women who worked at the company, a junior programmer and the financial controller. Both said that Margaret had repeatedly spoken to them of Robertson's incessant and unwelcome attentions and her deep dissatisfaction with Bill's failure to make him stop. Both women characterized Robertson as a borderline stalker, who would even follow Margaret to the bathroom. One of the women, by mutual arrangement, left work at the same time as Margaret so she wouldn't be "ambushed" by Robertson on her way to her car. Both women disclosed that they had counseled her simply to tell Robertson to "get lost" and "to keep his fat ass away." Margaret, however, was "much too timid" to even consider such a direct approach. Both women confirmed that Margaret had been increasingly apprehensive, even becoming physically ill, by having "that fat oaf" hounding her. Both remembered her throwing up in the women's rest room, apparently queasy from persistent anxiety. Both remembered her saying she was seeing a doctor for her ailments and had started taking sleeping pills.

The investigator then interviewed Robertson Hipple, who openly admitted his "love" for Margaret and how "bereaved" he felt over her leaving. He openly admitted that he had tried to call her, still hoping to "win her over." Robertson then mentioned how his boss understood his feelings and had encouraged him to be patient, that Margaret might eventually recognize his worth. "*Persevanti dabitur* is my motto," said Robertson brightly to the investigator. "All things come to him who perseveres."

Needless to say, the company attorney was not comforted by the investigator's report. He advised Bill that he and his company had a "high probability" of losing in court, possibly resulting in a judgment in the six-figure range, not including attorney's fees. Still befuddled by the fix he found himself in, Bill instructed his lawyer to call Margaret's attorney to see what he had in mind in regard to settlement. The initial demand was $150,000, which Bill's lawyer interpreted as a sign of weakness. Most plaintiff lawyers begin by setting a very high bar based on the principle that you can always negotiate down but never up.

The fact that Margaret's attorney had not filed the lawsuit, but had only threatened to file, seemed a shakedown tactic to Bill Trost. Bill's attorney, however, saw it simply as an opening jab in a gloves-off brawl. Sexual harassment suits, he explained, must always be defended vigorously. "If she wants that kind of money," he said, "she'll have to work for it." Bill did not understand what his attorney meant but soon would learn. "She's timid," said his attorney. "She'll settle for less." They counteroffered nothing and the lawsuit was subsequently filed.

Margaret's deposition was the first to be scheduled and lasted almost an entire day. Sitting in, Bill observed with growing discomfort as his attorney began his examination innocently but quickly progressed to questions of a most personal nature regarding her sexual history, personal hygiene, morality, and failed marriage. After hours of intense grilling, Margaret finally collapsed in tears, incapable of continuing. Her attorney put an end to the ruthless verbal assault and asked for a continuance. Bill Trost's attorney agreed, but with a sneer reminded Margaret that he had more questions, many more questions. Margaret left broken and distraught.

Bill felt dazed and ashamed by what he'd just witnessed. Unfazed, his attorney calmly recommended offering Margaret a token $5,000 to drop her suit. If she refused, he vowed to "get tough with her" when the deposition continued. Bill submissively agreed, though he was inwardly sickened by the conduct of his counselor. The offer was conveyed by phone to Margaret's attorney an hour later. The next morning, Margaret's attorney countered with a demand for $25,000. Sensing the upper hand, Bill's attorney recommended holding firm at $5,000. Guilt-ridden and remorseful, Bill Trost refused and directed

158 □ CHRISTOPHER EIBEN

his attorney to accept the counteroffer. Privately, Bill told friends he would have and should have paid more. He later learned to his regret that Margaret Semple continued experiencing emotional problems long after the case had been settled.

□ □ □ **COMMENTARY AND ANALYSIS**

Sex and work, Sigmund Freud observed, drive virtually all human behavior. When the two overlap, as in the two preceding cases, the volatile mix can explode into controversy and litigation. Laws addressing sexual harassment in the workplace have indeed created a whole new battlefield in the war between the sexes. In addition to the obvious emotional consequences, accusations of sexual harassment pose significant financial exposure to employers. Judgments routinely exceed $1 million, and the cost of defense can be as high as $250,000 for cases that go to trial. Today, more than 20,000 sexual harassment cases are filed each year and the numbers are growing.

As with so much legislation, the intentions behind sexual harassment laws were pure and noble. Sexual harassment in the workplace is a very real problem that reportedly has affected 40 to 60 percent of all working women. Sexual harassment differs from harmless flirtation or sincere social interest. It is offensive and threatening to women, often forcing them to leave jobs and triggering serious psychological and health problems. Make no mistake—legitimate cases of sexual harassment surpass fraudulent ones by at least a factor of ten to one. Most complaints arise from the base, thoughtless, and shameful behavior of men towards women.

With the possible exception of contested divorce, no area of civil litigation today is more ugly, painful, or emotionally scarring than sexual harassment lawsuits, as both Margaret Semple and Harold Tupper would personally attest. Only the lawyers and fraudsters like Theresa Ivory come out winners; all other participants suffer horribly. What is so befuddling for many caught up in these kinds legal conflicts is that standards of behavior have changed so rapidly, accelerated by court decisions that continually redefine what is objectionable. When, for example, was the last time anyone has heard a "catcall," that approving two-note whistle that for decades had been an audible reaction of men to feminine beauty? Today, only old sailors and fools would dare whistle at a pretty coworker. Yet how does one differentiate between boorish and illegal behavior? When does a clumsy overture become an offensive proposition? Is it inappropriate nowadays to compliment someone's appearance or new clothes while on the job?

These questions are difficult to answer. In fact, what one person might shrug off as inconsequential another might litigate to the death as an egregious and compensable transgression. An appreciated compliment for one person might be a verbal assault for another. Outside the workplace, boorish behavior is only that, boorish behavior. On the job, however, that same behavior can be legally actionable, resulting in the offender and his (or even occasionally her) employer getting dragged into a costly and disruptive controversy.

Fifteen years ago, most sexual harassment lawsuits focused mostly on *quid pro quo* (this for that) misbehavior, usually involving a male supervisor pressuring a female subordinate for sexual favors in return for a raise, a promotion, or some other tangible benefit. In recent years, however, more cases have been filed alleging damages from a sexually hostile work environment that forced the complainant to resign. Those responsible need not be supervisors; a company may find itself liable for inappropriate behavior of rank and file workers when it knew, or should have known, about improper behavior and did nothing to stop it. According to recent higher court rulings, sexual harassment must be "based on sex" and also must be "severe and pervasive" for a complainant to prevail. Defining what is "severe and pervasive" can be problematic and often requires a jury to decide. Robertson Hipple's persistent attentions unquestionably affected Margaret Semple's health and peace of mind, though most women likely would have brushed off his oafish behavior without losing sleep over it. Unfortunately, there are no clear-cut guidelines to determine when offensive conduct rises to the level of "severe and pervasive" such that it constitutes actionable sexual harassment. Plaintiff lawyers might argue, "If you feel you've been sexually harassed then you have been," and many would be willing to take a case simply on that basis. With that in mind, employers are well advised, if not duty bound, to take remedial action if an employee complains about perceived sexual harassment.

Harold Tupper case

People understandably develop strong friendships and romantic attachments in the workplace. This simple fact places employers at risk. After all, relationships blossom but they also wither, and when they do, the law expects the employer to intervene and protect the estranged from harassment and the intentional infliction of emotional distress while in the workplace. Owners and managers, in particular, take enormous risks pursuing romantic attachments with subordinates. Considering the potential legal consequences, prudent managers today should limit their romantic pursuits to people outside the job. Had Theresa Ivory been as pure as a nun *and* truly interested in Harold Tupper, both he and the company would still have been exposed had their relationship soured, as relationships so often do despite the best initial intentions.

Of course, Theresa Ivory was not a nun but a conniving, immoral, and opportunistic enchantress. With the help of her predatory lawyer, she shamelessly manipulated the system for her personal financial gain. Though her case may have been somewhat unusual, the fact remains that many sexual harassment suits are based on false, trumped-up, or exaggerated accusations. Most cons and frauds are perpetrated on naive and vulnerable people like Harold Tupper. Though smart and accomplished, Harold blundered into Theresa Ivory's scheme because he was emotionally needy, muddling his otherwise good judgment.

All employers must be cautious when evaluating attractive and charismatic job applicants and put aside their positive first impressions. Harold Tupper's clouded judgment was not at all unusual. In the presence of feminine beauty, men sometimes don't think too clearly. Theresa Ivory so bewitched Harold that he failed to recognize obvious problems with her story, serious red flags he might have seen had he just been able to keep his eyes closed when first interviewing her.

Harold failed to follow one of the cardinal rules of background investigation: always be suspicious of personal histories that are difficult to verify; they are often deceptive and scripted to conceal something unfavorable. Harold should have postponed hiring Theresa until he verified her employment record and carefully examined the lengthy gap when she purportedly cared for her dying mother. Though it required a few extra phone calls, Harold should have tried to track down the owner of the "small electronics company" that supposedly employed Theresa before it went out of business. Had he checked, he would have quickly learned that no such company had ever existed. Furthermore, Harold should have questioned Theresa about caring for her dying mother. While honestly expressing concern and empathy, which might have entailed discussing subjects like hospice care and the complexities of caring for dying loved ones, he should have tactfully probed for more details, such as her mother's name and where she died. Such inquiries at a job interview may seem distasteful considering the sensitivity of the subject, but employers should worry less about decorum and more about the consequences of hiring someone dishonest. After all, it's better to be ill-mannered than ill-used.

Had he obtained her mother's name, Harold could have exposed Theresa's deception by searching the obituaries and vital statistics records to confirm her death. But even without going to such lengths, had Harold simply conducted a broad database search on Theresa Ivory, he would have been tipped off that she was no innocent. Her fourteen different addresses, multiple aliases (including "Honeysuckle Love"), her links to three different Social Security numbers, and the six judgments filed against her were all serious red flags concerning her character. Transposed numbers and other inputting errors occasionally result in misinformation about people. But the sheer magnitude of conflicting information and falsehoods found in the commercial databases concerning Theresa suggested deliberate deception. She likely provided the bogus information when applying for credit, filling out business forms, renting apartments, purchasing goods and services, leasing cars, and a host of other activities from which computer databases glean information. The civil judgments of record also suggested someone either very bad with money or very good at ripping people off.

Had Harold checked out Theresa by means of a thorough database search, he could easily have exposed her as untrustworthy in a follow-up telephone interview. What could Theresa Ivory possibly have said about the three Social Security numbers? What about her multiple, often concurrent addresses, particularly when supposedly caring for her mother? What about the judgments against her? Unfortunately, many employers are as bashful as teenagers when conducting job interviews, uneasy asking probing questions. Timid employers must toughen up and doggedly (though tactfully) probe for detailed and verifiable information before letting applicants in the door. Hiring someone on the basis of a pretty face and a perky personality is simply asking for trouble. Harold learned the hard way that employers should pay no notice to good looks until after they have thoroughly checked out an applicant's credentials and employment history.

Bill Trost case

In contrast to Harold Tupper's nightmare, Bill Trost's experience with Margaret Semple's sexual harassment lawsuit better illustrates the perplexing and painful issues courtrooms around the country wrestle with with every day. Margaret's case demonstrates that even well-meaning people can find themselves in a heap of legal trouble by being inattentive and unprepared. Robertson Hipple never intended to harass Margaret or cause her emotional distress, but he unquestionably (though unwittingly) did so. Bill Trost did not purposely subject Margaret to a hostile work environment, but his failure to act more decisively certainly created one for her.

When managers are aware (or should be aware) that harassment is occurring, their company can be held liable, particularly when the affronts are offensive, intentional, and repeated. Robertson Hipple's oafish conduct toward Margaret Semple was intentional and repeated, but was it offensive? Most would say no, but Robertson's conduct unquestionably offended the sensitive Margaret, creating a legal conundrum. Sexual harassment claims often hinge on the sensitivity of the woman (and occasionally man) involved. In other words, the harassed individual's experience and perception of the conduct as offensive is generally the ruling factor in establishing the legitimacy of a claim. Robertson's loutish behavior had the effect of interfering with Margaret's work performance and created (for her) an intimidating, hostile, and offensive work environment. When Margaret clearly and unambiguously complained to Bill Trost, he opened his firm up to liability by failing to intercede effectively on her behalf.

Yet what should have Bill have done? What can any employer do to minimize exposure to sexual harassment claims? Recent Supreme Court decisions have provided clear guidelines for establishing an affirmative defense for employers, who must do these four things:

- Adopt and distribute a written policy against sexual harassment in the workplace.

- Establish a complaint procedure and provide flexible avenues whereby aggrieved employees can express their concerns.

- Promptly, thoroughly, and impartially investigate all complaints.

- Take appropriate corrective and/or disciplinary actions when warranted following an investigation.

In addition to these four steps, employers can further minimize their legal exposure by having all employees sign an acknowledgment that they have read and understood the company's policy regarding sexual harassment together with the procedures for lodging a complaint. If an employee later fails to take advantage of any corrective opportunities provided by the employer, it will be difficult for that employee to prevail in any subsequent lawsuit. In addition to adopting and enforcing a clear and effective antiharassment policy, employers would be wise to require some sort of training to help employees recognize and comprehend impermissible conduct. Implementing these measures allows employers to argue that they took appropriate steps to censure harassment and discourage improper conduct from occurring in the first place.

Of course, Bill Trost had adopted no helpful policies and procedures, leaving his firm almost defenseless had Margaret's case gone to trial. All Bill had going for him was a vicious attorney bent on trau-matizing a vulnerable complainant into accepting a disadvantageous settlement. Indeed, Margaret had a strong case, but she lacked the emotional strength to push on to a judicial decision. At least in regard to sexual harassment suits, her case illustrates why "civil justice" is an oxymoron. Civility is notably absent in most sexual harassment cases, and the abusive use of legal proceedings too often overwhelms the pursuit of justice.

The most offensive and reprehensible attorney conduct invariably occurs during "discovery," the process before trial wherein each side has the opportunity to learn all the relevant facts and ascertain the truth of a case. Under current discovery rules, parties may seek not only evidence to support their case but also information that might reasonably lead to such evidence. With such wide latitude, discovery often devolves into blatant intimidation and psychic punishment. During marathon depositions, lawyers often try to torment under the guise of "fact-finding," a tawdry pretext for coercing people in a manner that would make the Grand Inquisitor blanch. Imagine for a moment being interrogated for hours about the quality of your erec-tion, frequency of intercourse, sexual vocalization, fantasies, past lovers, favorite positions, stamina, self-gratification, and other in-tensely personal subjects. Most of us would not endure such prurient scrutiny and would do whatever it takes to avoid it, even if it means dropping a just claim or paying an unjust settlement to avoid further embarrassment.

People unfamiliar with court proceedings often naively believe that truth and justice will ultimately prevail and the wronged will be com-pensated. In reality, emotional stamina and deep pockets play a larger role than truth and justice in the outcome of most sexual harassment lawsuits. The legal process can be excruciating for complainants and defendants alike. Zealous lawyers feel duty bound to inflict pain, dis-parage, humiliate, and even destroy on behalf of their clients. Indeed, the law is the only learned profession in which practitioners at times feel ethically obligated to hurt people. I have also seen attorneys with wealthy clients routinely and needlessly complicate the process, knowing that the other side lacks the financial resources to wage a long, costly legal battle. Nothing is more disheartening than dropping a good case or paying to settle a bogus one because of financial compulsion.

Indeed, money more than justice has become the life-blood of the civil judicial system. The staggering cost of defense frequently impels defendants to pay pretrial settlements that any impartial observer would describe as unjust and unwarranted. But faced with the enormous cost of going to trial, with attorney fees often climbing into the six-figures, defendants routinely pay five-figure settlements simply to cap their losses and stop the financial hemorrhaging. The sad truth is that every sexual harassment lawsuit, irrespective of the merits, has settlement value simply because of the high cost of mounting a legal defense. Indeed, it is usually cheaper to settle than to fight. Nowadays, only the most inflexibly principled and deep-pocketed defendants choose to pay their attorneys $100,000 rather than pay the complainant $20,000 to get lost. The financial pressure to settle before trial unfortunately creates conditions fertile for frivolous and fraudulent lawsuits. This maddening consequence of the high cost of legal representation makes implementing defensive strategies to avoid litigation doubly important for employers. Today, it is not enough to be legally right. Employers must also be strongly positioned to counter claims, thereby discouraging opportunistic lawyers trained to exploit faults and weaknesses. The goal is to discourage legal claims and to lower the settlement value of those cases that are filed.

Workplace banter, flirtations, and dalliances should not be considered a harmless part of work life; they are instead high-risk behaviors that employers should discourage. Prudent employers should plan ahead, monitor employee behavior, and intervene quickly if circumstances dictate. Not to do so can be very costly indeed.

□ □ □ CAUTIONARY TIPS

- Vague employment histories that are difficult to verify are generally deceptive or fraudulent.

- Employers should always verify an applicant's personal identifiers and be suspicious of those with multiple Social Security numbers, aliases, and frequent changes of address.
- Never date or romantically pursue anyone from work, particularly if you are in a position of authority.
- Lawsuits are often more about extorting money than rectifying a wrong.
- To avoid liability from sexual harassment claims, employers must do the following:
  - Adopt a strong written policy against sexual harassment.
  - Institute a complaint procedure that encourages employees to come forward if they suspect they or someone else has been a victim of sexual harassment.
  - Take every complaint seriously.
  - Quickly and thoroughly investigate each complaint.
  - Take appropriate corrective and disciplinary actions when warranted.
  - Try not to let the person who lodged the complaint become angry or frustrated, particularly when the investigation fails to corroborate the charges. A sympathetic and concerned approach defuses most emotionally charged situations.

CHAPTER 8

Cyberspace Investigations

□ □ □ **CASE #1—COLIN WEBHORN:**
    "E-COMMERCE FOR DUMMIES"

When his father finally retired from the family business, Colin Web-horn felt the change in leadership was long overdue. Colin had grand plans for Webhorn Ltd., a manufacturer of industrial components. He wanted to reconfigure the company for the new millennium by launching a major web presence with e-commerce capability, some-thing his tradition-bound father had never considered a priority. He'd stood by, itching with impatience, as his elderly father (who'd led the company into his early eighties, when the effects of a stroke finally forced him to relinquish control to the fifty-five-year-old Colin) largely ignored the explosion in digital technology that transformed business through the 1990s. Colin was no longer young himself, but fancied himself something of a technology-minded forward-thinker, and he spent much time developing his own modest personal com-puter skills (which he took considerable pride in) while he awaited his opportunity to take over the business. In anticipation, Colin had already registered an internet domain name, webhorn.com. He had also spent several months researching computer networks and the cost of servers. There would be some significant expenses, of course, but if profits increased by even a modest 10 percent, the initial invest-ment would be paid off in less than a year.

On his first day as CEO, Colin bought a new high-speed server/CPU and eight workstations that would be networked wirelessly; he envisioned that everyone at Webhorn Ltd. would ultimately be con-nected to the system, though initially only the accounting and sales staff would have computers. After completing the purchase, Colin also received an intimidating stack of operating manuals and other techni-cal documentation. "These are for your sysadmin," the salesman had said. Looking down at the eight pounds of technical manuals in his hands, Colin momentarily had second thoughts. He was proud of his own reasonably competent personal-computer skills, and he'd given what he considered a fair amount of thought to setting up a system that would serve his company's needs. But now, turning the manuals over in his hands, he realized that he might be exceeding the limits of his own computer knowledge. He wondered just how difficult it would be getting a company network up and running. The salesman quickly reassured him that it shouldn't be a problem. He did gently suggest, however, that Colin consider hiring someone with sysadmin experience, at least initially, to get the system running smoothly.

The new server and workstations were delivered and installed, but there were numerous problems with the hardware and the software. Even the word processing program was glitchy. Colin realized that hiring a competent system administrator was an urgent necessity. But how to find one?

Colin ran a classified ad for an experienced system administrator but failed to receive a single response. Not one. With his patience running out, in desperation he called Professor Carl Fulbright, chairman of the computer science department at City University, and asked if he could recommend someone. Professor Fulbright was not surprised that Colin had no responses. He explained that qualified system administrators were in great demand. His best students, the professor pointed out, often received a dozen job offers before even graduating. He could, however, recommend one very talented person—a young woman named Martha Hobart who had just received her degree.

Colin immediately called her, but was disappointed to learn that she had already accepted another position. Leaving no stone unturned, he asked Martha if she knew anyone else qualified who might be interested. She gave him the name of a former classmate, Malcolm Ledyard, a gifted computer programmer who hadn't graduated with the rest of their class. Ledyard, she explained, had left school just a few credits shy of his degree in computer sciences. She had heard that he was looking for work. As a college dropout himself, Colin was not overly concerned that this new prospect hadn't received his degree. After all, even the finest gems were once unpolished.

Before contacting Malcolm Ledyard, Colin called Professor Fulbright again and asked for his assessment of the young man. After an unusually long pause, the professor responded that, in his opinion, Malcolm was among the most brilliant students ever to attend City University, though his record certainly did not reflect this. Malcolm, he explained, had become so absorbed in the university's computer network that he had woefully neglected his core studies. Malcolm had dropped out last semester after taking an incomplete in two humanities classes. Colin then asked if the young man had the skills to implement an e-commerce strategy and to create an internet presence for Webhorn Ltd. The professor answered yes without elaborating. Would Malcolm make a good employee? Professor Fulbright again hesitated before answering, as if choosing his words carefully, and then gave a brief, equivocating endorsement, praising the young man's proficiency but expressing concerns about his "maturity." With very close supervision, the professor acknowledged, Malcolm might be successful. After thanking the professor, Colin hung up the phone, earnestly hoping he had found his sysadmin. In hindsight, he wished he had paid more attention to the professor's hesitations.

Despite his own casual style of dress, Colin Webhorn was taken aback when Malcolm Ledyard came in for a job interview two days later. The lanky young man looked like he should be dipped and sheared. His long hair needed washing, and his rumpled slacks and collarless shirt looked as if they'd been extracted from his laundry hamper. Four gold bands protruded from the cartilage of his left ear, and a black pearl Colin at first thought was a blood blister topped a pin piercing his right nostril.

Despite the young man's unconventional appearance, he obviously knew computers. When asked about his experience, he spoke laconically about several websites he had constructed, including almost all of City University's web pages. He also spoke of his thorough understanding of Linux, UNIX, Windows NT, and other operating systems. Colin then asked for Malcolm's opinion of the company's new computer and its adequacy for achieving his e-commerce plans. Without a word, Malcolm stepped over to the workstation adjacent Colin's desk. Like a self-assured virtuoso before a recital, he sat down, paused briefly as if concentrating, and then furiously started typing.

The monitor scrolled technical information about the system and its components, and the young man seemed to take in whole screens of data at a glance before commanding the system to do something else. It was an awesome display of technical and physical prowess. Colin knew he was in the presence of a true whiz kid, a high priest of the mysterious cult of computers.

Malcolm spun around on the swivel chair and with sublime insouciance informed Colin that the system would be adequate to do whatever Colin wanted. For security reasons, he suggested changing without delay the root password from the default configuration. Any user with root access, he cautioned, became the god of the network, with almost limitless power to go anywhere, read any file, and execute or modify any program. Root access represented the Holy Grail for crackers who undoubtedly would be scanning the company's system for vulnerabilities after the company had an internet presence.

Colin felt compelled to demonstrate he was not a complete neophyte by saying that he always understood the correct term to be "hacker," not "cracker." With just a hint of condescension, Malcolm explained that the common usage was wrong. Hacker properly referred to an expert programmer who could elegantly disassemble (or hack apart) code, changing the programming to expand the capabilities of a mainframe computer. A cracker, on the other hand, was the digital age's equivalent of a safecracker, someone able to break into computer networks for malicious purposes.

Colin expressed his doubts that a small company like his would ever become the victim of network intrusion. Malcolm told him that he should count on it. Most crackers employed war-dialers, scanners, and sniffer programs that automatically searched the internet for vulnerable servers. Any network system with certain ports left open, he warned, would eventually be exploited by crackers. Then, if a cracker succeeded in taking control of root, the system in effect would have a new supreme deity, able to change the source code for nefarious purposes. When Colin's face clouded with concern, Malcolm laconically reassured him that various security measures could be implemented to fend off the most common cracker attacks.

Though Colin found Malcolm's manner and appearance off-putting, he gave him the job anyway. Secretly, Colin intended to replace him as soon as he found someone more agreeable. During his first month as the company's system administrator, Malcolm performed admirably. He got all the workstations running, loaded new software and upgrades, educated various company users, and spent some time troubleshooting hardware problems. He also met with Colin occasionally to discuss the design of the company website. For Colin, their meetings were always strained and uncomfortable. He now had a firmer grasp of just how little he knew about computer technology, which made explaining his ideas and making informed decisions that much more difficult. The younger man offered few suggestions and little feedback while his boss rambled on nonsensically; Colin felt like a complete idiot around him. Though his sysadmin never said anything inappropriate or condescending, Colin interpreted his reticence as a form of derision.

Others in the office, however, did not have problems relating to Malcolm. Most of the staff were amused by his eccentricity and appreciated his helpfulness. For example, he helped the marketing director create a vendor database and an email address book of all clients and business prospects. He also helped the controller customize the company's accounting software to streamline billing. Despite his growing dislike for the young man, Colin grudgingly acknowledged his competence and work ethic. Nearly every day, Malcolm was still at his computer long after everyone else had left, typing away madly at his keyboard, though no one knew exactly what he was inputting.

About six weeks after he'd hired Malcolm, Colin came to work early and was surprised to see him asleep in his chair wearing the same wrinkled clothes from the day before. An acrid smell of unwashed socks and stale food permeated the air in his small, cluttered cubicle. Irritated, Colin loudly told him to wake up. Malcolm groggily opened his eyes, looked up at his boss, then yawned and stretched, seemingly indifferent to the rude awakening. Colin interpreted his behavior as blatant, premeditated insolence and instantly became enraged. In hindsight, he wished he'd controlled his emotions. Colin denounced Malcolm for his seedy appearance and then fired him on the spot. In truth, Colin had been looking for an excuse to get rid of Malcolm, having found someone else to replace him. Seemingly unperturbed, Malcolm got up without hurrying and slung his shabby backpack over his shoulder. He then explained he'd been up all night completing the company's website. "Check it out," he said coldly while heading for the door.

Later that morning Colin visited the company website, which was truly amazing, vastly exceeding his expectations. It was well organized, visually engaging, and informative, with numerous links to related subject websites. For the online catalogue, Malcolm had scanned various company marketing materials and then simplified them. The site also included point-and-click ordering capability with a shopping cart icon in the corner of each page. Colin was pleased to see a tasteful photograph of himself, something he had suggested but not expected, adjacent the company's upbeat mission statement. Malcolm had incorporated every one of his ideas and included many more useful features. Colin briefly felt ashamed for firing Malcolm after such exemplary work, but soon rationalized away his feelings. The young man simply did not fit in with the Webhorn corporate culture and thus had to go.

Pauline, the new sysadmin, started work two days later and began to familiarize herself with the computer system. She asked Colin for the root password, which of course he did not know. Without the password, she was effectively locked out of the system's control room. Becoming agitated, Colin told her to look around the workstation to see if Malcolm had written it down somewhere. She found nothing and Colin began to panic. Malcolm had him by the balls and Colin fully expected him to squeeze. At a loss as to what to do, Colin nervously instructed Pauline to call Malcolm and nicely ask him for it. He fully expected Malcolm to hang up on her, but was relieved to learn twenty minutes later that Malcolm had not only given her the password but also told her about several modifications he had made to the system. This information, she said, would help her immeasurably.

Later that week, working closely with Pauline and the marketing director, Colin sent out personalized emails to every client and business prospect, more than five hundred messages in all, announcing the company's new website and an introductory 10 percent discount program for every order placed online. Every email contained a link to the company's website. The promotion was an instant success, with almost 30 percent of all established customers taking advantage of the offer.

Prior to his dismissal, Malcolm had set up the system to generate an invoice automatically for all online orders and to record the transaction in the company's accounting ledgers. At first, everything worked perfectly. Two weeks into the promotion, however, one of the company's clients called to tell Colin that there obviously was a mistake in his invoice. What should have been a $2300 transaction had been billed at only $230. After some checking, the company controller discovered that the last sixty invoices all had the same misplaced decimal point, discounting every sale by 90 percent. No one could explain the glitch in the program.

The next day, another long-standing customer called Colin and indignantly told him he intended to take his business elsewhere, saying Webhorn Ltd.'s 25 percent increase in prices was simply ridiculous. Colin denied any such increase. The customer then read Colin an email he'd received, apparently sent at 4:32 A.M.:

"Effective immediately, Webhorn Ltd. is raising prices on its entire product line by 25 percent. Our low profit margins must be increased if I am to maintain the upscale lifestyle to which I have become accustomed. I thank you for your understanding and continued patronage."

Colin Webhorn, CEO

Colin strongly denied sending the message and stammered that it must have been a prank. Agitated, he hung up the phone and quickly checked the computer's message center. Between 4:22 A.M. and 4:24 A.M., the same email had been sent to hundreds of recipients—everyone in his internet address book. Aghast, he yelled for Pauline, who hurried into his office. Colin sputtered out what he'd discovered and demanded an explanation. Pauline quickly concluded that someone had gained unauthorized access to his user account. She then asked who else knew his password. "Malcolm!" thought Colin.

Colin berated himself for failing to change his password after firing Malcolm. The email prank must have been Malcolm's way of retaliating. But how could he prove it? Colin quickly changed his password from "chief" to "boss" and spent the rest of the day personally calling his best customers and sending emails to everyone else explaining that there was no price increase, that the company had been the victim of a prank. Colin had never been more embarrassed in his life. Without explicitly saying so, many customers clearly questioned his competence and doubted his explanation. Some had asked to speak with his father, not knowing he had retired.

The next morning, Colin arrived late to work feeling completely drained after a fitful night's sleep. When he walked into his office, several senior employees were waiting for him. He knew instantly something was seriously wrong. To his horror, he learned that in the early hours of the morning, another email message had been sent under his name and email address to hundreds of customers and vendors. The subject line read, "For your reading pleasure from Colin Webhorn." What followed was a repugnantly off-color joke. At the end of the email was a link to the Webhorn website, preceded by the words, "Click here for another good laugh."

Colin clicked the link and the screen switched to the company's homepage. Colin's photograph had been digitally altered, his face seamlessly pasted to a grotesquely fat woman's torso clad in a thong bikini. The "hit" counter indicated hundreds had visited the website since the previous day.

Investigation and Aftermath

After disconnecting the server and calming down somewhat, Colin called the police. A detective came over and interviewed Pauline and Colin, taking some notes, but expressed doubts that the police department had the investigative capability to handle the case. He agreed, however, that the former sysadmin was the likely culprit. Colin pushed him to arrest him and search his home computer for evidence of wrongdoing. The detective said that he would discuss it with the prosecutor, but cautioned that without evidence linking Malcolm to the intrusion, not much could be done.

The authorities did essentially nothing, though the police investigator did speak with Malcolm, who indignantly denied any involvement whatsoever. Malcolm pointed out that he'd helped the company's new sysadmin after being fired. The investigator later told Colin what he'd learned and observed that the help Malcolm had offered seemed inconsistent with someone intent on retaliation. The detective patronizingly advised Colin that a prosecutable case depended on facts, not suspicions, and as far as he could see there was no evidence against Malcolm.

Unable to let it rest, Colin hired a private investigator recommended by the company's attorney. The investigator, a man highly experienced in network intrusion detection, met with Colin and Pauline to discuss the case. Colin first asked him how Malcolm could have gained access to the system, considering that both his personal password and the root password had been changed, to "boss" and "administrator" respectively, passwords Malcolm could not have known. Shaking his head, the investigator explained that Malcolm could well have used a password cracking software program readily available on the internet, likely one with a dictionary tool. Passwords found in the English dictionary usually take only seconds to crack.

The investigator tried to lessen Colin's self-reproach for his poor password selection, saying Malcolm most likely gained access through a "backdoor" or hidden account. As sysadmin he had ample opportunity to set one up and likely did so. The expert then recommended what he called "nuking the entire system from high orbit," which meant completely reformatting the disk drives and reloading all the software programs, the most prudent approach considering that the system had been compromised. None of the backup disks, he pointed out, should be considered clean. Essentially, Webhorn Ltd. had to start all over to be absolutely certain the cyber-vandal had been completely purged from the network.

Feeling violated and wrathful, Colin made it his life's mission to get Malcolm. He paid the private investigator a large retainer and implored him to find something linking Malcolm to the cyber-vandalism. The investigator began his inquiry by contacting Professor Fulbright at City University, who was not surprised to learn what had happened. He disclosed that Malcolm had been under suspicion the year before for hacking into the registrar's computer files and changing the star quarterback's grades to avert his academic suspension. Malcolm had also been suspected of posting some outrageous graffiti on the university's electronic bulletin board. Despite widespread rumors, the school could never prove Malcolm's involvement in either incident. For that reason, Fulbright had felt uncomfortable mentioning anything about them to Colin when he'd called for a reference.

The investigator then interviewed the university's sysadmin, who provided still more disconcerting information. For two years, Malcolm had been a student volunteer helping to administer the university's computer network. The sysadmin acknowledged that Malcolm was a prodigy who probably knew more about the university's computers than he did. Malcolm, he said, was also a tireless worker who didn't think twice about pulling an all-nighter if interested in a project. Though the sysadmin liked and admired the young man, he conceded that Malcolm had "a dark side." Apparently, Malcolm had been hosting an IRC (internet relay chat) site on the university's network for several months before the sysadmin had discovered his clandestine bulletin board and shut it down. However, he hadn't brought this to the attention of any City University officials, thinking it would also have reflected very badly on himself. This secret IRC had been a gathering place for serious crackers who would post their exploits and share their attack methods with other like-minded enthusiasts. The members of this quasi-club apparently called themselves the Gods of Guile. After discovering the secret IRC site, the sysadmin took away Malcolm's privileges and administrative responsibilities and banned him from the system. Malcolm had dropped out of school shortly thereafter.

The investigator asked the university's sysadmin if any of the IRC sessions had been archived or preserved in the system. The sysadmin said that there might be some on the backup tapes from the year before and promised to run off hard copies if he found anything.

The investigator then asked him for the names of Malcolm's friends and accomplices, anyone who might know more about his hacking activities. The sysadmin, unfortunately, wasn't particularly helpful on this subject. Everyone in the cracker community used aliases or handles; connecting a real name to a cracker's handle was a difficult assignment. For obvious reasons, maintaining anonymity is standard operating procedure for those dedicated to computer mischief. The sysadmin, however, did suggest contacting Martha Hobart, another former student who had worked closely with Malcolm on improving the university's website. The investigator recalled that she had been the one who'd recommended Malcolm to Colin for the system administrator position.

Martha Hobart at first was tight-lipped about Malcolm's activities as a cracker, but after appealing to her sense of decency she finally opened up. Though she considered Malcolm a friend, his apparent cyber-attacks had clearly crossed the line. Martha enjoyed a clever exploit, such as Malcolm's changing the grades of the quarterback, but she had no tolerance for criminal mischief. Martha had never been a member of the Gods of Guile nor had she participated in any cracker activities. As a conscientious student, she'd focused instead on grades and career aspirations. She knew a little about the cracker underground, however, including several IRC sites where Malcolm and his friends hung out online and shared their secrets. She also told him Malcolm's cracker handle: Cyberfiend.

Back at his office, the investigator went online, searching electronic bulletin boards for the postings that undoubtedly had steered thousands of visitors to Webhorn Ltd.'s vandalized website in the hours before discovery and disconnect. Bravado and grandiosity often impel crackers to broadcast news of their exploits. With so many hits on the website counter, Malcolm had obviously gotten the word out electronically. Using a Usenet search engine, the investigator found several postings in less than a minute by simply typing "webhorn.com" in the subject line. On several hacker bulletin boards, someone with the handle "Computer Lad," using a City University email address, had posted the following: "Check out the homepage at Webhorn.com for a funny exploit. This won't be up long so hurry and pass the word!"

178 □ CHRISTOPHER EIBEN

The investigator called City University's sysadmin and told him about the postings. Both agreed that Computer Lad was likely Malcolm hiding behind a spoofed university email address to maintain his anonymity. The sysadmin had suspected all along that Malcolm had been using the university's network to set up the occasional bogus user account, but there was not much he could do about it. Having been a privileged user with root access, Malcolm knew dozens of ways into and around the system. Even if the sysadmin nuked the entire network, the backup tapes were suspect, so there was no point in even trying to get rid of him. Hardened firewalls were not an option because the university depended on the open flow of information.

On the subject of backup tapes, the sysadmin informed the investigator he had printouts from several IRC sessions from the previous year. Apparently, most of the chat sessions had been erased, but the Gods of Guile had overlooked a few. The sysadmin promised to deliver what he found by courier. The investigator persuaded the sysadmin not to confront Malcolm, not wanting to tip him off that someone experienced was on his tail.

The IRC session printouts revealed the breadth of Malcolm's skills at network intrusion. His postings as "Cyberfiend" were insightful and technically brilliant, and identified a broad array of network vulnerabilities, some of which were unknown even to the celebrated security watchdog CERT, the Computer Emergency Response Team at Carnegie Mellon University. Many thousands of hackers and crackers roam cyberspace, but only a few dozen reign supreme. Malcolm clearly was among the elite. Reviewing the printouts, the investigator also learned the names of some of Cyberfiend's associates—crackers with handles like Wonker, Droid, Boodyboy, and Slyder—which would soon prove helpful.

The investigator went undercover in cyberspace posing as a teenager with the handle "Visigoth," thinking a barbarian warrior would have cachet with young male crackers. Visigoth began lurking around the active hacker IRC sites identified by Martha Hobart. Most of the bulletin boards had been abandoned, undoubtedly replaced by others hosted on some hacker's home computer. After a week on the case, Visigoth's break came when he bumped into Boodyboy and Slyder at one of the chat sites. With heart pumping, Visigoth immediately typed, "I hear Cyberfiend pulled off a sweet exploit last week . . . anyone know about it?" Slyder took the bait and expounded on the Webhorn website attack, having obviously seen firsthand the altered photograph of Colin. Boodyboy chimed in by adding it had been a sweet act of revenge. Webhorn, he added, had messed with the wrong guy. Cyberfiend had made the company pay big-time. Visigoth kept them chatting, drawing out details, while continuously saving their cyber-dialogue to his own hard drive.

After he logged off, the investigator then printed a hard copy and prepared an affidavit identifying the circumstances behind the IRC session, including time, place, etc. He then took it to a notary, swore an oath as to its accuracy, and signed it. Later that day, he had Martha Hobart sign a sworn affidavit saying she had personal, firsthand knowledge that Malcolm Ledyard had used the handle "Cyberfiend" in email and IRC communications. Copies of the IRC printouts from City University were also attached as supporting evidence. The investigator then took what he had to Colin Webhorn and the Webhorn company attorney, convinced he had enough evidence to persuade the prosecutor to move forward on the case.

Later that day, the prosecutor reviewed the investigative findings and obtained a search warrant from a sympathetic judge. That night, police investigators raided Malcolm Ledyard's apartment, confiscated his personal computer, and took him into custody for questioning. They found Malcolm's room unexpectedly neat and tidy. While they boxed up and carried out his computer, disks, and personal papers, Malcolm remained relaxed and unconcerned despite being hand-cuffed. At the police station, he remained perfectly calm and stead-fastly maintained his innocence during prolonged questioning. He waived his right to speak with an attorney, saying repeatedly that they were mistaken, that if anyone had been wronged it was he, not Colin Webhorn and his company.

Exasperated by Malcolm's smug attitude, the detective eventually produced the IRC transcripts and the affidavit from Martha Hobart, and for a moment Malcolm's composure cracked slightly. His eyes got big and his mouth briefly opened in surprise. But then he recovered and continued to deny any involvement in the Webhorn attack. He also denied ever using or going by the handles Cyberfiend, Computer Lad, or any other name for that matter. At about midnight, after more than an hour of questioning, an expert who'd been examining Malcolm's computer came into the room and whispered in the investigator's ear. The investigator's face grew very red at the news. Watching his accuser intently, Malcolm smiled slightly as if reading his mind. The investigator told Malcolm that he was free to go, but advised him that their investigation would continue. Malcolm got up and walked out without saying another word.

Two experts had carefully examined Malcolm's computer but found absolutely nothing incriminating. Generally, even deleted files and email messages can be recovered at least partially from a hard drive, because the delete command merely makes available the disk space used by a "deleted" file without actually erasing that file's contents. Malcolm's machine, however, was as clean as the day it had been shipped from the factory. He had obviously used an "overwrite" or data-destruction software program such as Scorch, Shredder, or BCWipe to eliminate all traces of his cracker activities. Even his email address book had been emptied and wiped clean. The only files still on his computer were a few poorly written essays in the word processing program. His internet browser had only three bookmarks—quick links to several evangelical Christian websites. None of the disks and notebooks seized from Malcolm's apartment contained any evidence of wrongdoing.

The prosecutor declined to press charges against Malcolm, knowing a conviction would be next to impossible. The private investigator spoke with a few young men supposedly connected with the Gods of Guile hacker group but got completely stonewalled. The hacker community had obviously circled the wagons around its own.

Colin Webhorn hired a public relations firm to help repair the damage and restore Webhorn Ltd.'s reputation. All told, the company lost only about $50,000. Webhorn's clients for the most part were very understanding. About a half-year later, Colin unveiled a new website for Webhorn Ltd., but this time the server had a firewall with both active and passive intrusion detection capabilities. Malcolm Ledyard got a job with an internet security firm and became an acknowledged expert in the field. Webhorn Ltd. was never attacked again, though Colin did receive a cryptic email message from an internal account that simply said, "Stopped by to say hi." The message was signed, "Cyberfiend."

Pauline immediately installed the latest security patch to the communications software. After that, Webhorn's online doors and windows remained secure, though the detection software occasionally indicated hackers had tested the locks and rattled the knobs, usually in the middle of the night.

□ □ □ **COMMENTARY AND ANALYSIS**

Like unsuspecting lemmings, businesspeople have marched lockstep into the "new economy" over the past decade, embracing e-commerce and launching web-based initiatives while largely oblivious to the risks and exposures that accompany them. Colin Webhorn is just one of many who learned the hard way that computer communications technology has been oversold as a sure route to business success. The internet's virtues have been praised with almost religious fervor, but its vulnerabilities deserve just as much attention. Multitudes of businesses have been needlessly damaged, including many that have yet to realize it. As we become increasingly and overwhelmingly dependent on computers and computer networks, we also become more vulnerable to cyber-vandals and cyber-criminals.

The problem stems from the very nature of the technology. Though only around for a generation and still relatively primitive, personal computers now pervade our economy and have become increasingly interconnected. The vulnerability of computer networks arises from the simple fact that the PC was first designed as a stand-alone device, providing a single individual unhindered access to his personal data and programs. Security was never a concern because that individual was unlikely to damage his own computer or misuse what was on it. Connectivity between personal computers began slowly, starting less than twenty years ago with Bitnet, a group of loosely linked university mainframe computers that allowed trusted users to share information. From this primitive beginning came the explosion of the World Wide Web and the link it provides among millions of computers and computer networks.

Before long, what had originally been stand-alone programs and applications created for stand-alone personal computers—including operating systems, spreadsheets, word processors, email functions, and eventually internet browsers—were tightly integrated. The phenomenal success of Microsoft and other software companies was only enhanced by the evolving ease with which files could be exchanged among PCs. But expanding connectivity also created new risks. Even when the best way to share files among PCs was to pass them along in versions saved on diskettes, viruses that impaired a computer's software were already a burgeoning risk. Once computers became connected, they ceased to be under the sole control of owners who naturally protected their computers and the data on them. But with the vastly expanded connectivity enabled by the growth of the internet and World Wide Web in the 1990s, computer owners began sharing their data both consciously and unconsciously with strangers in cyberspace—some of whom have criminal intentions.

These circumstances have greatly increased the risk of external attacks upon individuals, such as Colin Webhorn, and upon our entire economy, as we've become increasingly dependent on these systems. The most notorious attacks can be indiscriminate and wide-ranging, such as those launched by individuals disseminating malicious code—computer viruses and worms—which can cause enormous combined losses. Attacks can also be narrowly focused, such as Malcolm's assault on the Webhorn network. Defending against these assaults requires constant vigilance, along with countermeasures and strong safeguards to protect networks. Unfortunately, current defenses are not particularly robust, in part because of the built-in character of operating systems originally designed to serve unnetworked individual users. Some might even say "internet security" is an oxymoron, because connecting with the internet is inherently risky. Indeed, the only surefire way to protect a computer network is to keep it disconnected from the internet entirely, something impractical in today's business world.

There are legions of crackers prowling the internet looking for vulnerabilities to exploit. Even well-funded, technologically savvy organizations are vulnerable to their attacks. One legendary exploit occurred on September 19, 1996, when Scandinavian hackers penetrated the CIA's website, altered its homepage to read "Central Stupidity Agency," and imbedded links to pornographic websites. Notorious cracker Kevin Mitnick once penetrated the North American Air Defense Command (NORAD). These events are now part of hacker lore—but it often seems as though not a month can go by without the proliferation of yet another destructive worm or virus. If the most security-conscious agencies on earth can be exploited, what hope is there for the average company?

According to recent surveys by the Computer Security Institute, the number of computer crimes and security breaches has grown every year, resulting in cumulative losses in the billions of dollars. More than 90 percent of large corporations experience some sort of intrusion every year. More than 10,000 websites are vandalized every year, despite widespread implementation of security measures. What is scary is that the security surveys understate the full magnitude of the problem. Detected intrusions are only the tip of an enormous iceberg. For example, in 1999 the U.S. Defense Information Systems attempted 10,000 network intrusions of Department of Defense facilities, of which 88 percent were successful. Only 4 percent of the intrusion attempts were detected, and only 5 percent of those detected attempts triggered any kind of defensive response. In the last ten years, companies and organizations have rushed to build networks and connect them to the internet. Many of these networks are profoundly vulnerable, the equivalent of leaving household doors ajar while away on vacation. For these unprotected networks, it is only a question of time before a cyber-criminal enters and ransacks what is there.

The cracker community expends an enormous amount of time and effort scanning the internet for unprotected networks. Notoriously relentless, crackers are willing to put in more time looking for vulnerabilities than most businesspeople are in implementing good security. In particular, they look for low-hanging fruit—those networks easiest to exploit. Despite their mystique, very few crackers are brilliant programmers like Malcolm; most are simply amateurs ("script kiddies") using software they've downloaded from the internet to pursue their aims, including automatic scanning tools and programs for launching exploits after vulnerabilities have been identified. Anyone who can master word processing software can learn to be a hacker. The threat from these "script kiddies" increases daily as their numbers grow and their arsenal of scanning and attack tools becomes more sophisticated and more widely available.

Colin Webhorn was mistaken thinking that crackers would be uninterested in his company's network. Such systems are precisely what crackers look for to stage exploits and launch attacks against more secure targets. Sophisticated crackers often mask their identity by "looping" and "weaving" through multiple sites in various countries. By electronic impersonation, or "spoofing," they disguise their computer to look like another in order to gain access to networks with sensitive data. Unwitting businesses then get dragged into criminal investigations for misdeeds launched from their unprotected systems. In the future, businesses may even find themselves liable for damages for negligently failing to secure their network. The sad truth is that, as is the case with most criminals, only the stupidest and most careless crackers are ever identified and caught. The really good ones, like Malcolm, move unnoticed among networks without leaving a trace.

The cracker culture, which promotes sharing programs, skills, and even password accounts, compounds the risks to network newbies unaware of cyberspace dangers. Mentoring others and sharing information are part of the honor code of the online underground. Crackers also love to crow about their exploits, posting their trophies on electronic bulletin boards and boasting about them in real-time chat rooms. A compromised system can become a popular objective, and copycat attackers appear out of nowhere to hit it again and again, almost like ants alerting the nest to incite swarms of its fellows to feast on the vulnerable.

Cracker tools that use brute-force computing power are potent threats to targeted networks. Network security, of course, hinges on keeping unauthorized users out, and passwords are the first line of defense. Unfortunately, nearly every computer network in America has authorized users who, out of laziness or laxity, choose passwords that are too simple to provide any real security. In fact, poor password selection is responsible for most network intrusions. Numerous programs exist—including Crackerjack, Npasswd, and Cracklib to name a few—which can crack passwords by simply guessing, at rates as fast as 50,000 guesses per second. If the password is a five-letter word that can be found in the dictionary, these crack programs can usually discover it in a matter of seconds. On the other hand, a password made up of eight randomly chosen upper- and lower-case letters, numbers, and punctuation extends the necessary computing time from minutes to centuries. Understandably, security-minded companies should require all authorized users to choose complex passwords and penalize those who do not.

After successfully "guessing" a password, an intruder can use the system under the guise of a legitimate user. Once in, someone clever can then install hidden "trapdoors" for later access and even install surveillance or "sniffer" programs that operate in a stealth mode very difficult to detect. They can steal data, vandalize programs, delete files, spray digital graffiti, and generally wreak havoc on a system. Disruptions and damage can be catastrophic if the intruder accesses the system's root directory on the network, possibly through an open account or default configuration. These are usually the consequence of an inattentive or inexperienced sysadmin. Alterations to the system on the root level can be enormously difficult to identify and correct, even for the most skilled computer specialists.

The unpublicized truth is that most sysadmins are simply not qualified for the growing complexities of the job. With the explosive growth of the internet and the enormous increase in the number of computer networks, the number of experienced sysadmins has not kept up with the demand. Colin's difficulty finding a capable sysadmin was not at all unusual. Even established companies paying generous wages and providing lavish benefits have trouble finding competent people for this role. Just ten years ago, most sysadmins had many years of experience and intimate knowledge of UNIX and other sophisticated operating systems. Today, the average sysadmin is likely a recent college graduate and former PC jockey who may know very little about network operating systems, security, and intrusion detection. Small companies that have only recently gone online are particularly vulnerable because, not knowing any better, clueless newbies are more prone to hire clueless administrators.

The richly paneled board rooms of corporate America are still largely populated by technologically illiterate business veterans. Many of these normally cautious captains of commerce and industry have entrusted the very future of their enterprises to young, inexperienced techies in the effort to fit out their businesses for e-commerce. These business leaders have invested fortunes in complex networks that haven't a prayer of generating profits anytime soon, but have exposed their companies to many new risks, including some they will never fully understand. Why have so many sensible and experienced businessmen headed down this risky path? Fear drives many of them—fear of being left behind in the "new" economy, and of being perceived as anachronistic in a time of tectonic change. But history shows that disasters often ensue when emotions drive behavior, particularly group behavior.

The downside of the explosion in connectivity is still unclear, but the exposures are enough to make any security-minded individual break into a cold sweat. Our country's increasing dependence on internet technology to run critical infrastructures—including banking, power distribution, and transportation systems—provides obvious targets for cyber-terrorists. In the wake of 9/11, we can be certain that political agendas drive the actions of at least some crackers and cyber-vandals. Undoubtedly, cyber-terrorists have been responsible for spreading some of the malicious code infecting networks nationwide. Why bother hijacking airliners when it is possible to bring down a company, possibly even a country, with well-planned, coordinated cyber-attacks on key vulnerabilities in its computer-driven infrastructure?

So what should sensibly paranoid businesspeople do in the face of such exposures? First and foremost, they should slow down. For many companies, there is no reason to rush into building computer networks with all the bells and whistles. Computer networks should be constructed incrementally, with an eye toward security, and the single best security measure is to hire a competent sysadmin. A competent sysadmin can help define a reasonable network program with specific, cost-effective objectives. In doing so, the "crown jewels" of a company—its proprietary, financial, personnel, and other highly sensitive data—should generally be segregated from dial-in access entirely. Electronic sales and fund-transfer capabilities should be the last components implemented, and only after the network has been obsessively evaluated for vulnerabilities and security shortcomings.

Unfortunately, businesses often rely on the judgment of sysadmins without really testing their competence or verifying that their reassurances regarding security are credible. Most upper-level managers simply do not have the training or experience necessary to check that the company's network is reasonably secure. It is my professional opinion that sysadmin incompetence and negligence result in most of the serious network problems for companies. Even those who know better are often too lax, because safe computing requires unremitting vigilance and effort. Cyber-vandals enter vulnerable networks daily through ports left open and holes unpatched. After a system crashes, it is often difficult to determine what caused it. Equipment malfunctions and software bugs are often hard to distinguish from an intruder's mischief. With so much at stake, the security work of sysadmins must be tested and tested often, both by someone internally and by experienced outside experts brought in for that very purpose. Remember, vulnerabilities are always easier and cheaper to eliminate before a system has been compromised. Reduction of crime opportunities is always the first step in crime prevention, whether in cyberspace or the bricks-and-mortar world.

The principles behind good network security would require a book in itself, but a few basics will help empower managers, notwithstanding their limited expertise in computer technology. To reduce risks, companies should do the following.

Find and hire superlative sysadmins and treat them like princes (or princesses). Despite their value in the job marketplace, (or perhaps as a result of it), too many companies hire inexperienced sysadmins and then fail to show them the appreciation and respect (particularly the respect doled out via payroll each month) commensurate with the importance of their responsibilities. A disenchanted and resentful sysadmin is not someone you want controlling your company's network. Give sysadmins the time, tools, and support they need to do their jobs well, including outside technical expertise and a generous budget for continuing education. Like medicine, computer technology evolves rapidly, and sysadmins must be encouraged to keep up with those changes.

Sysadmins must make security their highest priority. Furthermore, companies should insist that sysadmins make recommendations on the best ways to improve network security. Security, after all, depends on a committed state of mind; it's an active process that goes well beyond the simple installation of firewalls and virus protection software. Like homeowners checking locks and latches on their doors and windows, sysadmins must seek out vulnerabilities in the networks they administer. They should be suspicious of any inquiries they might receive regarding the network and its specifications. When stymied, crackers often resort to "social engineering," using clever pretexts to get sysadmins and others who know the system to reveal information that can help them gain unauthorized access. Some crackers are highly skilled at impersonating software engineers and trusted insiders, using plausible pretexts to persuade sysadmins to reveal passwords and network specifications.

Establish written policies and protocols for updating software. These should spell out how the network's software programs must be updated with patches applied as soon as they become available from the relevant software publisher. Often, CERT will discover new network vulnerabilities and then recommend specific security patches to eliminate them. Yet many sysadmins fail to monitor or implement CERT's recommendations, irresponsibly leaving known security holes in their systems. Of course, crackers also read the CERT bulletins regarding software flaws and use them as guideposts to attack other similarly based systems. Time is of the essence after vulnerabilities have been identified. Managers must direct sysadmins by making it policy that all published updates and software patches must be promptly installed. Virus software updates in particular must be installed the day they become available. Managers should require sysadmins to maintain a log of all update activities, including entries for scheduled communications with software publishers verifying that updates are current. Periodically, outside experts should be hired to review the sysadmin's logs, without prior notice, to ensure compliance with company policies.

Install surveillance software. Make employees aware that the company reserves the right to monitor all network activity in the interest of maximizing productivity. Every company should institute written policies that the computer network and all software and data on it belong to the company. Every employee should be required to sign an acknowledgment that he or she understands this company policy and accepts it, and that they should have no expectation of privacy whatsoever when using company computers. Such a blanket restriction may sound extreme, but in addition to improving security, it can help companies curb productivity losses resulting from employees wasting time on the internet and reading/sending personal emails. I believe that more than 95 percent of all mischief and misuse of a company's network can be eliminated simply by *announcing* the installation of surveillance software After detecting unauthorized or inappropriate employee computer use, the company should take the offending employee aside to remind him or her of the company policy. The first offense or two should be treated leniently, with only a warning, followed by a written memo addressed to all employees reminding everyone of the policy and calling attention to the detected violation without identifying the transgressor. Treated courteously and diplomatically, most employees will understand and accept restricted use of the company network.

Sysadmins should be immediately notified when an employee leaves the company. This should apply whether the employee leaves voluntarily or involuntarily. The sysadmin should immediately close that employee's account and privileged access to the company network.

All companies should frequently and diligently audit their security systems. Sysadmins should be made aware at the time of hire that outside experts will be periodically engaged to probe the network for vulnerabilities and security flaws. The best computer security firms ("white hats") use proven cracker techniques—everything from ping sweeps to social engineering—to compromise a system. Sysadmins should be informed that this regular (though unannounced) exercise is intended to support the sysadmin's efforts to implement and maintain good security. This sets a high bar from the beginning, and periodic network attacks serve as a pragmatic test of a sysadmin's capability and work ethic. True professionals will rise to and enjoy the challenge by trying to make the network as impregnable as possible. Of course, sysadmins should always be recognized and rewarded whenever these staged attacks are successfully thwarted.

Network security and computer-crime prevention take on heightened importance for every organization with an internet presence for another very important reason: governmental authorities are often at a huge disadvantage in combating cyber-criminals. Without the necessary expertise, many police departments are completely ineffective in investigating cyber-crimes. Some departments do not even respond to reports of network intrusion and computer vandalism. Criminals naturally become emboldened when they know their chances of being caught and prosecuted are about 10,000 to 1. The truth is that computer crimes are enormously difficult and costly to investigate. Skilled hackers always cover their tracks, making them very difficult to trace. There is a dearth of skilled investigators capable of solving computer crimes, mirroring the shortage of sysadmins capable of preventing computer crimes. Small wonder then that the vast majority of network intrusions resulting in the theft or destruction of property go unreported, and those that are reported almost never lead to a criminal conviction.

Despite the enormous risks and huge costs, companies continue to rush to transact business on the web: electronic commerce is the wave of the future, and the basic medium of this commerce will be electronic funds transfer. Will this lead to greater prosperity and productivity, or are we creating an economic equivalent to the little pig's house made of straw? Time will tell. Those companies, however, that build their electronic houses with bricks (good security and sound policies) will better keep the wolves at bay.

□ □ □ **CAUTIONARY TIPS**

- Businesses should secure their computer networks, taking for granted that crackers are trying to breach their security.
- Treat network security as an active process requiring continuing education and frequent software and hardware upgrades.
- Treat superior sysadmins like royalty, and pay them according to their responsibility for guarding an organization's electronic soul.

"It Pays to Be Paranoid"

Thomas Jefferson once observed, "Constant vigilance is the price of freedom." This insight from 200 years ago seems even more relevant today. We live in an era of outlandish expectations, animated by a pervasive cultural craving for personal wealth and instant gratification. Our money-driven culture fosters a growing belief in personal entitlement, magnified by a declining sense of personal responsibility. In this mad scramble for individual gain, where many embrace an anything-goes approach to secure an advantage, businesspeople and investors must be ever vigilant if they are to remain free from conflict, complications, losses, and lawsuits.

Everyone has heard the adage, "money can't buy happiness," but few truly believe it. Advertising and media bombard us with the opposite message: having money is good and spending it is even better. To be honest, money scares me. As an investigator, I have seen its corrosive effects on those who have it and on those who don't. Having seen legions of monetarily ambitious people wracked by worry and burdened by legal troubles, I now fervently believe that embracing the accumulation of wealth as one's principal goal assuredly leads to a fretful and unhappy life.

The unfettered pursuit of money implies a willingness to take advantage of others, triggering an insidious and ultimately self-defeating domino effect: taking advantage of others leads to quarrels, quarrels lead to angry disputes, angry disputes lead to heightened anxiety, heightened anxiety to sour negativity, sour negativity to unhappiness, and unhappiness to an unfulfilled, thoroughly wasted life. From my professional perspective, the obsessive pursuit of a "good life" culturally defined by acquisitiveness and material consumption means the senseless pursuit of an illusion, one exposed by the proliferation of conflicts clogging our justice system. Too many of these countless fights are triggered by the venal behavior of people who just had to have more. In truth, the *good* life doesn't mean having things; it means living free from conflict and worry. Certainly, the many embattled Enron millionaires would now agree. How many of them would prefer their comparatively carefree and uncomplicated lives before the yachts and mansions? I suspect most if not all.

Don't get me wrong: there is nothing wrong with having or earning money, even lots of it, so long as it arises from worthy ambition. The corrosive effects of money occur when it becomes the primary goal, rather than the happy consequence of worthwhile work. Those businesspeople contributing the most to our society by way of innovation and service almost never obsess about making money. They focus instead on turning their ideas into realities, and many get wealthy in the process. Though ambitious, they are not motivated by greed.

Having our peace of mind is finally much more valuable than having money. Yet how do we protect and preserve our peace of mind? How do we nurture harmony and happiness? In his 1796 farewell address, George Washington counseled his countrymen to "avoid entangling alliances." Though referring to nations, Washington's admonition certainly applies to individuals as well. Our most consequential choices involve who we let into our lives. Who we choose to be with and include in our lives will largely determine whether we will be happy or miserable.

I have a simplistic view of humanity as a spectrum ranging from very good to very bad. For roughly half of all people, their positive attributes outweigh the negative, and for the other half, their negative attributes outweigh the positive. To increase the chances for well being, people should minimize contact with the lower half—and avoid altogether the bottom 10 percent, those twisted, unsafe creatures who simply do not care about the welfare of others. It's this bottom 10 percent that everyone needs to worry about in earnest.

The depraved scoundrels and the selfish connivers described in this book certainly fall within this ignominious grouping. All of them, as we have seen, could have been identified and avoided before they caused their mischief. To avoid the worst kind of people, however, you must first expect them and know they exist, fully capable and perfectly willing to take advantage of you. In short, it pays to be paranoid! Most of the victims in this book were decent people oblivious to their peril. Their generally positive and hopeful outlook often blinded them to lurking risks and dangers, ironically making them more vulnerable, more likely to experience painful ordeals never at all anticipated.

Avoiding the worst is just one half of the equation in preserving peace of mind. The other half requires finding and connecting with the upper 10 percent of humanity, those whose positive attributes vastly outweigh their negative. This select group includes the gifted and upright, those more interested in giving than getting, hard-working and loyal people with an overriding ambition to accomplish good. Special people gravitate to special people. They recognize the value of spending their time with those they like and admire, and the inherent waste of spending it with those they loathe and fear. Good people enrich the lives of other good people. They make life worth living.

Success in business and investing, achieving good results *and* peace of mind, presupposes the avoidance of conflicts and controversies—particularly legal controversies. Those who mingle with the bottom 10 percent of humanity will undoubtedly suffer the consequences. But even good people sometimes find themselves in legal disputes simply from carelessness and inattention to risks. In business, one should always hope for the best but prepare for the worst. Everyone should remember that the ladder of success is unstable—one wrong step and you just might come crashing down.

□ □ □ **FINAL CAUTIONARY TIPS:**

- In a world of legal tripwires, always think about where you step.
- Implement a stringent compliance program and remain alert for changes in the employment and regulatory laws peculiar to your business or industry.
- Be fair, honest, decent, scrupulous, and consistent in your business dealings with others, and you'll be less likely to get entangled in conflict or become a target of miscreant behavior.

- Unless absolutely necessary, never take someone into your confidence in matters that might embarrass or hurt you if ending up in the wrong hands.

- Just because someone confides in you doesn't mean you must confide in him or her. A confidence is a gift, and a gift confers no rights. Similarly, gifts should not be bestowed on just anyone.

- Never say or write anything in anger. Always wait until you cool off before responding. A letter written or words said in anger often puts a weapon in the hands of an enemy.

- Always be careful what you put in writing, particularly in emails that can be duplicated and broadcast to the entire world. Written words often have legal and contractual consequences.

- Surround yourself with good, capable people and avoid those who are not.

- Develop close relationships with excellent, experienced attorneys. Consult with them early and often on business matters of importance.

- Avoid all avoidable trouble.

- Always be prepared to defend yourself against unavoidable trouble.

ABOUT THE AUTHOR

As a licensed private investigator and business consultant, **Christopher Eiben** has helped hundreds of clients on cases involving financial fraud, workplace accidents, negligent hiring, sexual harassment, regulatory issues, mergers and acquisitions, and executive recruitment. He is a certified legal investigator and an active member of the National Association of Legal Investigators, the Association of Certified Fraud Examiners, and the National Council of Investigation and Security Services. He can be contacted through his website, Ipry.com.